Encyclopædic dictionary of mountaineering

This dictionary is primarily intended
to serve as an educational
reference work both for the
enthusiast and the interested
layman.

The subjects dealt with include
the architecture of mountains
down to minute features; the
techniques and equipment used to
climb rocks, snow and ice; the
history of mountaineering and the
geographical and geological aspects
of mountains.

A comprehensive general index
gives easy cross reference for terms
which have several meanings, or
several alternative names; and also
for the many continental terms in
common usage, some of which
are still preferred to their less
romantic English equivalents.

Other appendices give details of
English language guide books,
technical publications, magazines
and important club journals.

The Matterhorn.

Encyclopædic dictionary of mountaineering

Peter Crew

Constable London

Published by
Constable & Company Ltd
10 Orange Street
London WC2

Copyright © Peter Crew 1968
First published 1968

SBN 09 455650 4

Illustrations by R. Brian Evans
Designed by Graham Bishop

Printed in England by
C. Tinling & Company Ltd
Liverpool, London and Prescot

Contents

Diagrams

Photographs

Appearing between pages 64-65

Introduction

This dictionary has been written to serve as a reference book. It can be used by the novice and interested layman, who is looking for definitions and meanings, to enable him to understand the jargon and string of confusing technical terms which have grown up with British mountaineering in the past hundred years or so. As in many pastimes, expressions and phrases used in mountaineering today read and sound like a foreign language to the uninitiated. It is interesting to note that the number of terms in this dictionary is almost double the number in Robin Collomb's original work, published in 1957. The first aim of this dictionary, therefore, is to elucidate this language, though experienced mountaineers will still find much of use and interest to discuss in their inactive moments.

The dictionary does not claim to put before the reader who wishes to improve his climbing ability every technique used to climb mountains. Techniques are too varied and numerous, and although some definitions necessarily sound instructional, this work is no substitute for a good instructional book (see Appendix III).

In the case of names of mountain and cliff features I have tried to be precise without misleading the reader —a difficult task because precise definitions have so many exceptions. Many features are complex, often consisting of combinations of several minor features, and an infinite number of variations of this kind are possible but must be omitted in the interests of the basic essentials.

A number of straightforward

geographical and geological terms
have been defined in an abbreviated
form and only as far as they are
applicable to the world of mountain
climbing. This means that in many
instances the wider sense of the term
has been ignored.

The temptation to widen the scope
of this work by including a selection
of names of mountain ranges and
places has been avoided. Such a
selection would be necessarily
incomplete and is already covered in
a greater depth than would be
possible here by the *Standard
Encyclopædia of the World's Mountains*
by Anthony Huxley.

An apology is due for the great
number of cross-references. Many
of them are due to the variety of
dialects spoken in the widely
separated mountain regions of our
own country and to the introduction
of the French, German and Italian
equivalents of some of our British
climbing terms, for in a sport like
mountaineering foreign words and
phrases are soon adopted and fall
into general use. Not all the
important terms have been given in
the foreign equivalents, for this
would have meant compiling another
book, but the few that are given
make the beginnings of a useful
foreign mountaineering vocabulary.

Acknowledgements

The author wishes to express his thanks to Robin Collomb who provided the initial inspiration for this work by his original work, *A Dictionary of Mountaineering*, published in 1957, and who has contributed many helpful suggestions towards the selection and treatment of terms appearing in this Dictionary.

Thanks are also due to Brian Evans for providing the excellent illustrations; to Martin Boysen, Mick Burke, Dougal Haston and José Luis Fonrouge, members of the 1967/8 British Cerro Torre Expedition, for many helpful suggestions and criticisms; and to Bernard Amy and Sylvia Metzeltin for assistance with continental terms and preparation of the General Index.

A.A.C. American Alpine Club, founded in 1902, with headquarters in New York, is the national body in the United States of America responsible for representing American mountaineering interests. Publishes an annual journal. There are several important regional clubs in America, with larger memberships than the national body.

Abseil. (*German.*) A method of descending over steep rocks, snow or ice by sliding down a fixed double rope. Abseiling is common practice in mountaineering, for it saves time during long descents, allows retreat when unforseen difficulties arise and, in fact, is often the only possible way of descending some mountains. The principle of abseiling is to pass the rope around the body, or through a special friction device, so that the rate of descent can be controlled. In the classic method the abseil rope is passed under one leg, across the chest and over the opposite shoulder. A less painful method is to sit in a leg harness, with the rope passing through a karabiner on the harness instead of under the leg, and then over a shoulder as before. Modern methods make use of the leg harness and a special friction device, around which the rope is wrapped in a special way. Many such devices are available (see *Descendeur, Brake-Bar, Figure-of-8*) and they permit faster and more easily controlled abseiling. Diagram p. 13.

Abseil Loop. A short piece of rope or tape whose ends are knotted or spliced to make a loop. The loop is used to make a leg harness in which the climber sits when making an abseil. The circumference of the loop is generally seven to eight feet, depending on the size of the climber and the method used to make the leg harness. Diagram p. 13.

Abseil Piton. Generally used to describe any piton from which an abseil is made, but more specifically to describe a special piton which has a forged ring instead of a fixed eye. The ring sometimes avoids the necessity to use an abseil sling.

Abseil Point. A ledge or a position on a mountain from which a climber commences an abseil. Also the fixing point (spike, chockstone, piton or tree) to which the abseil sling is attached.

Abseiling technique and equipment.
(1) *Classic Abseil* (2) *Abseil with leg harness*
(3) *Descendeur made from karabiners*
(4) *Allain Descendeur* (5) *Peck Descendeur*
(6) *Figure-of-8.*

Abseil Rope. The rope used by a climber to make an abseil. This is normally either a long rope used double, or two ropes of equal length tied together. By using a double rope the climber can retrieve the rope from below, after making an abseil, by pulling one end of the rope. When using two ropes knotted together care has to be taken to ensure that the correct end is pulled, otherwise the knot may jam at the abseil point.

When climbing difficult mountains, where abseiling is more likely to be of a necessity than a convenience, climbers habitually use a double rope for climbing and thus, conveniently, have the requisite ropes for abseiling. Since one normally abseils down a route which is also used for ascent, abseil points are usually available at convenient distances, so that two climbing ropes of 150 feet each will nearly always suffice. Diagram p. 13.

Abseil Sling. A short loop of rope or tape, which is tied onto the abseil point to ensure that the abseil rope runs freely when it is retrieved and to avoid leaving expensive karabiners behind. The abseil rope is threaded through the abseil sling. Abseil slings are normally made from a spare length of rope carried for the purpose, the exact length being cut off as required. In the Alps one often comes across abseil points with several slings attached, left behind by previous parties and usually in various states of decay. It is a wise precaution to renew every abseil sling, however good it may appear.

A.C.C. Alpine Club of Canada, the national mountaineering club of Canada, founded in 1906, largely due to the influence of English emmigrants who brought with them the spirit of exploration which had begun with mountaineering in the Alps. The traditional headquarters of the club are at Banff. Publishes an annual journal.

Acclimatisation. The process of becoming accustomed to climbing at altitudes where the oxygen is thin. The proportion of oxygen in the air at high altitude is virtually the same as that at sea level, but the pressure of the gases that make up our atmosphere decreases as the altitude increases. Thus at 10,000 feet, which is approximately the altitude at which acclimatisation becomes necessary, the air is 'thinner' than at sea level, whilst at 25,000 feet there is barely sufficient oxygen to enable a person to breathe. The process of acclimatisation consists of allowing the body to adjust itself slowly, to enable it to function satisfactorily in the new environment. Attempting to climb at high altitudes without a period of acclimatisation normally results in mountain sickness (q.v.).

The proceedure of acclimatisation is very simple up to altitudes of around 18,000 feet. The climber starts modestly with short days, climbing peaks of between 10,000 and 12,000 feet high and gradually working up to longer excursions and greater heights. For the ascent of a 14,000 foot mountain in the Alps the normal period of acclimatisation for people of good health and average constitution is about 10 days. The period of acclimatisation can be proportionally less for people who have more experience of climbing at these altitudes, and, in fact, people who climb or live habitually at these altitudes can reach a permanent state of acclimatisation.

For altitudes above 18,000 feet, as in the Himalayas, acclimatisation takes far longer but is a similar proceedure. One notable feature about Himalayan acclimatisation is that there is a point of deterioration, around 21,000 feet, above which it is no longer possible to acclimatise for higher altitudes for more than very short periods. This again largely depends on the individual circumstances. Above heights of say 23,000 feet oxygen apparatus is normally used to diminish the effects of altitude. However, even artificial oxygen only effectively reduces the conditions to those of a few thousand feet lower and great feats of endurance are needed to reach the summits of the highest Himalayan peaks.

Ace of Hearts. A very small and thin French piton for use in the smallest cracks. The name derives from the heart shape of the blade.

À Cheval. (*French*.) A method of climbing or traversing a smooth narrow ridge. The climber sits astride the ridge and makes progress by gripping the sides of it with the knees and legs while the hands press downwards on the ridge ahead. The technique is a last resort as a method of climbing ridges, being painful and slow, but can be used on steep or horizontal and rock or ice ridges. Diagram p. 16.

Active Rope. The length of rope between a moving climber and another climber responsible for belaying the former. When the leader is climbing, the rope paid out by the second is active; when the second is climbing, the rope taken in by the leader is active.

Aiguille. (*French*.) A steep pointed mountain, usually with sharp and distinct outlines. Nearly half the high mountains in the French Alps are prefixed *aiguille*.

Air Mattress. An inflatable mattress, of rubberised cloth or plastic, used to provide extra comfort for camping and bivouacing.

Alp. An Alpine pasturage and upland grazing land, sometimes cultivated, but generally used to nurture cattle, sheep and goats. The livestock is driven onto the Alps in the late spring and is brought down to shelter in the valleys before the winter snowfalls. Primitive chalet living-quarters for shepherds and herdsmen can be seen on all Alps.

Alpenstock. The forerunner of the modern ice-axe. In the early part of the nineteenth century the shaft was anything up to five feet long, with the adze forged vertically in the same manner as the blade of a wood-cutting axe.

Alpine Climbing Group. Founded by a group of leading British Alpinists in 1953. The principle objective of the group is to make up to date information of Alpine climbs available to its members by publication of an annual journal and a series of guidebooks to the more popular Alpine areas. In 1967 the A.C.G. was merged with the Alpine

Climbing a rock arête à cheval.

Club, but still retains its own functions and a high standard of climbing for membership.

Alpine Club. The first Alpine Club formed, founded in London in 1857 by John Ball, T. W. Hinchcliffe, E. S. and T. S. Kennedy, W. Matthews, Alfred Wills and others. The Alpine Club now has a large membership, with offices in London where meetings and lectures are regularly held. Publishes a bi-annual journal and a series of guidebooks to Alpine areas.

Alps. The name applied to the range of mountains extending across Western Europe from the French Mediterranean coast to central Austria. The highest summit in the Alps is that of Mont Blanc (15,771 feet) on the Franco-Italian frontier. Mont Blanc was first climbed in 1786 by Dr. Paccard and Jaques Balmat. (See *Four-thousander*.)

Alternate leads. A method of climbing steep rocks or ice whereby two climbers lead alternate pitches of a climb, instead of the more usual method of one person leading the whole climb. The technique obviously requires two climbers of similar ability, each capable of leading any of the problems which may arise. Because alternate leads, or leading through as it is often called, avoids the need to change belays and equipment, it is a very fast method of climbing and as such is used mainly in the Alps.

Altimeter. A modified aneroid barometer which shows the height above sea-level. The readings are only approximate because of changes in atmospheric pressure and thus can only be of limited use.

A.M.C. Appalachian Mountain Club, the oldest domestic walking, rambling and climbing club in the United States of America, founded in 1876. Publishes an annual journal called *Appalachia*.

Amphitheatre. The name adopted by climbers to describe a small rocky cirque from which a number of climbs are usually possible.

Angle Piton. An American chrome-molybdenum piton, made with a rounded U-shaped blade. The eye of an angle piton is made through both sides of the U pressed together. Angles are made in varying sizes and are designed to fit medium size cracks up to $1\frac{1}{2}''$ wide. The smallest angles are called Baby Angles; the $\frac{3}{4}''$ angles are called Standard Angles. Diagram p. 94.

Anorak. A light outer garment, with a hood attached, for protecting the upper part of the body from wind and rain. Usually made from closely woven cotton, with a silicone water repellent finish, or from a completely proofed nylon cloth.

Approach March. The walk or scramble from a departure point in the mountains to the foot of the mountain proper, or cliff face which is to be climbed. The end of an approach march is usually the beginning of roped climbing. In Britain, approach marches are seldom long or serious, except in some areas of Scotland. Normally good paths can be followed and the distances involved are relatively short compared to Alpine approach marches.

In the Alps, however, approach marches can be as long as seven hours, involving difficult climbing and glacier travel. In any high altitude range of mountains, which can normally be only climbed by expedition tactics, approach marches may take many weeks. In this case food and equipment for the duration of the expedition are carried by mules or porters hired specially for the purpose. Expedition approach marches usually end at Base Camp, which is then used as a central point for the rest of the expedition.

Arête. (*French*.) A ridge. Still used widely by British mountaineers, both in the true sense of the word, and also to describe a sharp rock or ice edge between two faces. The angle of an arête can be anything from horizontal to vertical and even overhanging. The size of an arête can vary from that of a major mountain feature to that of a small detail on a rock outcrop. Photographs 1, 8.

Arête Faîtière. (*French*.) Understood to refer to the main or most important (topographically) ridge of a mountain. It is frequently used in the French Alps to distinguish between main and subsidiary ridges of the same mountain, particularly if these two ridges lie parallel or close together. More often than not, the arête faîtière is the watershed of the mountain.

Artificial. A word used to describe graded rock climbs or mountaineer-ing routes which can easily be abandoned, once embarked upon, by a traverse onto an easier route. Many British rock climbs are artificial because of grass ledges which lead across them at various levels, linking up with easier ground. A route is also said to be artificial if it lies parallel or close to an easier route which can be reached by relatively easy climbing. The concept of artificiality changes from crag to crag and area to area, depending on the size of the crag, the degree to which it has been explored and how often it is frequented. Obviously outcrops will be developed to a far greater extent than crags in mountain areas, with a greater percentage of artificial routes. However, the fact that a particular route is artificial need not necessarily detract from its charm, and many such routes are worthwhile doing.

Artificial Aids. Those items of equipment which enable climbers to ascend steep rocks or ice which cannot be climbed by conventional methods and techniques. They include slings, chockstones, nuts, pitons, wedges, expansion bolts, skyhooks, etc., although some of these articles may be used to facilitate the practice of conventional climbing without their being classified as artificial aids, except by mountaineering purists. Generally speaking they may be said to be used as artificial aids only when they are applied in climbing to provide artificial hand and footholds, to make artificial stances and to enhance the practice of artificial climbing. Most climbers accept the use of pitons as belays, since these are a fundamental safeguard and do not materially aid the climbing of the route, but to the purist all pitons and the like are artificial aids, whatever purpose they serve.

The ethical viewpoint regarding the use and definition of artificial aids varies from area to area and even from climber to climber and is one of the most controversial subjects in climbing. Rock climbers in Britain and America have particularly strict codes of ethics, which has resulted in them being amongst the most able rock climbers in the world. Diagrams pp. 76, 118 and photograph 5.

Artificial Climbing. Climbing steep rocks and ice using mainly artificial aids. The easiest kind of artificial climbing is when the aids are used merely as hand and foot holds, but most artificial climbing demands the use of étriers and a special rope technique.

The classic method of artificial climbing is to use two ropes. The climber progresses by fixing a piton then climbing up an étrier on this piton as high as possible. One of the ropes, passing through a karabiner on this piton, may be used to give tension to assist the climber whilst fixing the next piton. The second rope can then be clipped into the next piton and used as a kind of pulley to help the climber move up. This method of artificial climbing is unsatisfactory for several reasons, mainly because it requires active co-operation from the second man for giving tension, which can be a very tiring business. A slight improvement is for the leader to use a cow's-tail to give himself support on one piton whilst fixing the next and for the leader to operate the pulley system when moving up to a new piton.

A much more satisfactory method, developed in America, is now becoming popular. The leader uses only a single rope for protection and avoids the use of tension by more sophisticated étrier techniques. The principle difference with the American technique is that the rope is only clipped into a piton once the climber has established himself on it and is satisfied that it is sound. This is very important on the harder artificial climbs, since it reduces the potential distance of a fall should the piton come out. Using a single rope makes the actual procedure of artificial climbing less confusing and therefore faster and it also allows the second rope to be used as a trail rope, which is indispensable on long hard climbs, where extra equipment may have to be pulled up from the second.

Most British and Alpine artificial climbs normally have all the pitons in place and so the ascent of such climbs is quick, even for a party of two. On the longer artificial routes in North America and on some of the modern Alpine routes, where pitons have to be inserted and removed, it is usual for two ropes of two climbers to do the climb with the lead rope inserting the pitons and fixing ropes, whilst second party follow, recovering the equipment and perhaps carrying the bivouac equipment.

There are many specific artificial techniques and items of equipment described individually (see *Étrier, Cow's-tail, Trail Rope, Tie-off, Hero Loop, Top-rung Moves, Pitons, Expansion Bolts, Skyhooks, etc.*). Diagram p. 20.

Artificial climbing over a series of roofs. The climber is using double-rope technique with a trail rope. Note the method of sustaining balance by hooking the back foot in the étrier.

Avalanche. A falling mass of rock, snow or ice. Avalanches are caused by a wide variety of circumstances, most of which stem from the melting of snow and ice during the daytime and in summer. Typical avalanches are as follows: masses of rock and earth dislodged from a steep hillside by heavy rain, soft snow sliding on steep grass slopes, wet snow or powder snow sliding on a harder surface of snow or ice, slabs of snow compacted by the wind sliding on softer snow, ice from séracs or hanging glaciers collapsing, stones and ice dislodged by melting and building up into an avalanche. Avalanches are usually serious for any climber involved and it is a wise precaution to make a careful study of all the likely conditions and to avoid avalanche prone areas.

Avalanches often assume immense proportions, carrying thousands of tons of rock and debris and may thus work havoc, destroying forests, roads and even villages.

Avalanche Cone. The mass of material deposited where an avalanche has fallen. Because the debris is compacted by the force of the avalanche, the cone remains long after other signs of the avalanche and in places where avalanches occur frequently (i.e. in couloirs) the cone may become a permanent feature. Avalanche cones at the foot of couloirs often fill the bergshrund and provide a convenient access to such couloirs.

Avalanche Cord. A long length of thin cord attached to a skier's waist and used when crossing a particularly avalanche prone area. The cord is intended to assist rescuers in finding skiers caught in an avalanche. In practice few people use an avalanche cord and the technique is mainly used by rescuers, when there is a likelyhood of further avalanches.

Avalanche Wind. The high wind produced by a large avalanche, which sometimes causes destruction at a considerable distance from the avalanche itself.

Bachmann Knot. A more sophisticated and more effective version of the prusik knot, where the prusik sling is wrapped round one side of a karabiner and the prusik rope. The karabiner can be used as a handle and for moving the knot up the rope.

Back and Foot. A method of climbing chimneys. The back is placed against one wall of the chimney and the feet against the other, so that the body is in a right-angle position. Upward progress is made by raising each foot and the back separately, using the hands pressed against the wall which supports the back, to allow upward movement of the back. In chimneys narrower than the length of the climbers leg, the technique can still be used by keeping the knees bent. In this case, the feet may be used alternately on the same wall as the back, to assist upward movement. Diagram p. 30.

Back and Knee. A method of climbing chimneys which are too narrow to be climbed by Back and Foot. The back is placed against one wall of the chimney, the knees against the other, so that the body is in a sort of sitting position. Upward progress is made by raising the back and knees alternately, using the hands and feet pressed against either wall to steady and ease the upward movements. This technique is very strenuous and painful and is only used as a last resort, when the chimney is too smooth to allow the use of wedging techniques.

Backing Up. A colloquial term for the Back and Foot and Back and Knee methods of climbing chimneys.

Back Rope. A technique sometimes used by the second man on a rope, to protect himself across a difficult or unprotected traverse, where there is any likelyhood of a pendulum in case of a fall. The method generally used is to pass a rope through a running belay at the beginning of the traverse and as the second progresses the leader pays this rope out, whilst taking the normal rope in. If only one rope is available, the same effect can be achieved by passing the rope through the running belay and the second man clipping a karabiner over the active rope. In either case, the worst that can happen in case of a fall, is that the second will be suspended in a V of rope, from which recovery should be relatively easy. When the back rope is no longer required, the second man unties from the rope, and pulls it through the runner.

Balaclava. A soft woollen helmet which can be worn as a cap or pulled down over the ears and lower part of the face to give protection from wind and driving snow.

Balance Climbing. A technique used for climbing smooth rocks, where there are few positive holds for the hands and where the climber maintains a position of balance by careful choice of hand and foot holds. Progress is made by 'walking' up the rock face, using the hands to maintain balance. Balance climbing is not usually strenuous but requires a high standard of technique and nerve, being more insecure than other techniques.

Balance Move. An upward, downward or lateral movement of the body in rock climbing in which balance is the key requirement.

Balling Up. The adherence of soft wet snow to the soles of boots or the spikes of crampons. The condition of balling up is uncomfortable for climbing, because it upsets balance and makes movement more strenuous. On steep slopes it can be dangerous, as it greatly increases the tendency to slip. The caked snow should be removed by frequently banging ones ice-axe against the boots or crampons and for long stretches of snow in balling up condition, crampons should be removed altogether. The climber should beware of avalanche conditions when balling up occurs.

Bare Glacier. A glacier whose surface is free from moraine and moraine debris. The névé and upper reaches of all glaciers are bare, but the lower reaches of most glaciers have some moraine covering.

Barres Rocheuses. (*French.*) Rock barriers. The term is normally used to describe bands of steep smooth rocks which are encountered on approach marches and which bar access to the snowline, glaciers or a higher section of the mountain.

Basalt. A fine-grained igneous rock, forming a lava flow or a minor intrusion. It is generally a very compact rock and the jointing is often perfect and columnar. Basalt is rarely suitable for climbing, but it often occurs in bands, or in the beds of gullies and must be treated with care.

Base Camp. A term used in expedition climbing to designate the principal camp, at or near the foot of the mountain to be climbed, from which the attempts to climb the mountain are made. Base Camp is nearly always made at a relatively low altitude and in pleasant surroundings, so that the climbers can recover there in between assaults on the mountain.

Bastion. The name occasionally applied in Britain to a prominent buttress or a smooth section of a cliff which gives a rock climb.

Bed. The back of a gully. Usually applied to a fairly level part of a gully between two pitches, or to a steep clean section between smooth walls.

Bedding Plane. The surface which separates one layer of sedimentary rock from another. In gritstone and sandstone, bedding planes are usually horizontal, giving good flat holds. If the bedding plane slopes towards the climber, most of the holds will be sloping; if the bedding plane slopes away from the climber, most of the holds will be incut. If the bedding planes of a cliff face are close together the climbs will be relatively easy; if they are far apart, then there may be steep and difficult stretches of rock to surmount.

Belay. As a noun, belay is used as a general term to describe all the possible objects (spike, chockstone, tree, piton, etc.) to which one can attach a sling and karabiner to provide static or dynamic security (see *Running Belay*).

As a verb, to belay is to tie oneself, as a stationary member of a roped party, to a firm anchor point (belay), either with the inactive climbing rope or with a sling and karabiner, in order to secure oneself and to safeguard another moving climber.

Belaying is the primary safeguard in mountaineering and its practice is universal. Its purpose is to safeguard all climbers in a roped party who are not moving and to provide security for the moving leader or second (see *Waist Belay* and *Shoulder Belay*). In the case of a fall, the belayed climber theoretically can not be pulled off the cliff face and is therefore in a position to stop the fall by holding the active rope. However, in reality it is possible for belays to break under stress, or for the belay to become useless by a change in body position caused by a fall (i.e. in the case of a leader falling onto a running belay and the belayer being lifted higher than a spike belay). Thus it is wise to have several belays to ensure maximum protection in all circumstances. Sometimes only poor belays are available, but anything which offers some degree of security should be used. (See *Jammed-knot Belay* and *Psychological Belay*).

Belaying in the Alps is often disregarded on straightforward rock and snow climbs in order to save time, and members of a roped party move together whenever their capabilities allow. The result is that more difficult rocks in the Alps are climbed without the use of belays in this country, but that a number of makeshift belays—such as running the active rope over a projecting rock in a pulley fashion— are frequently employed (see *Direct Belay* and *Simultaneous Movement*). Diagrams pp. 120 and 123.

Belay in Opposition. A belay made by using two or more opposing belay points. Quite often a single belay may only be good for a pull in a certain direction. By choosing another belay which is good for a pull in the opposite direction, and linking the two together, a satisfactory belay may be obtained.

Belay Length. A rope sling, usually of a diameter equal to the climbing rope and about 10 feet in length, reserved specially for belaying purposes.

Belay Seat. A piece of lightweight nylon material, approximately one foot square, sewn firmly to a loop of tape and used to provide a comfortable seat for belaying on long and overhanging artificial climbs. In emergency, a belay seat can be used for a bivouac, or for rescuing an injured climber from a cliff.

Bench Mark. A mark made by a surveyor on a permanent object, usually a rock wall or a concrete pedestal, to indicate a point whose height above sea-level is known and recorded. The Ordnance Survey use a horizontal bar above an upward pointing arrow for this purpose and on maps the site of a Bench Mark is indicated by the letters B.M. and the height in feet.

Benighted. The condition of being stranded unintentionally on a mountain after dark. This can be the result of miscalculations in time, unforseen difficulties and delays caused by bad weather. Normally the term benighted is applied to a party intending to return to the valley or a Base Camp, but it is also applied to a party intending to bivouac at a predetermined spot, but being prevented from reaching it (see *Bivouac*).

Bergshrund. (*German.*) The last big crevasse across the head of a glacier, usually separating the glacier from a rock wall, or steeper slopes above. There is no equivalent word in English. Because of the abrupt change in angle between the glacier and the headwall, the upper lip of a bergshrund may be many feet above the level of the lower one and, for this reason, a bergshrund may be very difficult to cross. Snowbridges and avalanche cones often span the gap early in the season, but are liable to collapse later in the year. Because of the difficulties in crossing bergshrunds, they often form an important feature of a climb. Photograph 7.

Bivouac. A temporary encampment in mountain country, or high on a mountain. Intentional bivouacs are necessary on routes which cannot be climbed in a day and parties intending to bivouac will normally carry special lightweight equipment for cooking, sleeping and shelter. A bivouac made under compulsion is called a forced bivouac (see *Benighted*).

Bivouac Sack. A lightweight waterproof nylon bag, or simple tent, used to give protection during a bivouac. Bivouac sacks vary greatly in design, but usually hold 2 people and weigh less than 2 lbs. Because a bivouac sack is completely waterproof it needs some kind of simple ventilation system and very careful use to avoid extreme condensation. Diagram p. 26.

Bivouac Site. A place on a mountain chosen for a bivouac. The most important factors are that the site should be sheltered from wind and any possible stone-falls or avalanches. Sometimes it is possible to use a small cave, or an overhanging rock, for shelter, but usually bivouac sites are a ledge at the foot of a rock wall which can be improved by building a low stone wall as a wind break. On snow, it is usual to dig a snow hole, or to use a small crevasse. In certain snow conditions it may be possible to build an igloo, or at least a snow wall for shelter.

Bivouac Hut. Usually a small wooden or aluminium hut, holding from 2 to 6 people, and placed on a long popular Alpine climb which needs 2 days or more for its ascent. These huts are usually financed and built by the Alpine clubs in the area concerned. There are a few bivouac huts in Scotland, which are mainly intended for use as emergency shelters in bad weather.

Black Ice. A thin layer of ice formed in the beds of gullies by alternate melting and freezing; also old ice exposed when an ice field retreats. Black ice is extremely hard and difficult to cut. Its dark colour comes from the colour of the underlying rocks showing through, or from the gravel and dirt embedded in it.

Blade Piton. A name used generally to describe any piton which has a flat blade, usually with an eye at right-angles to the blade. (See *Lost Arrow* and *Offset*.) Diagram p. 94.

Bleausard. (*French.*) A colloquial term for Parisian climbers who frequent the sandstone outcrops at Fontainbleau. The term is often used in a slightly derogatory sense, to imply that a climber is a very good outcrop climber but not a good mountaineer.

Blind Crack. A hair-line crack (q.v.) or any crack which ends after a short distance and cannot be used satisfactorily for inserting a piton. (See *Bottoming*.)

Bluff. A large jutting rib of ground in mountainous country, steep at one end and tapering gently at the other.

Boiler Plates. Smooth convex slabs or rock, often undercut and overlapping, usually found alongside a retreating glacier.

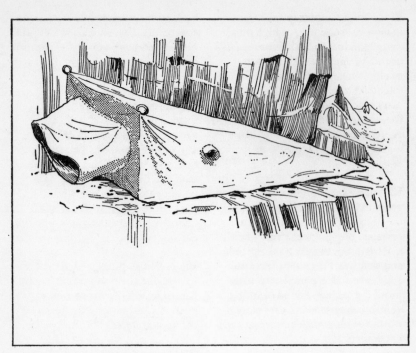

A typical bivouac sack and site.

Bollard. An upstanding rounded piece of rock, often useful for a belay point.

Bomb-bay Chimney. A term used mainly in North America to describe a chimney cutting through a roof, so that on climbing the chimney one is suspended above space and sometimes partly hanging in it!

Bong-bong. An American chrome-molybdenum piton, made with a U-shaped blade, which looks like a cow-bell sawn in half, and is intended for use in wide cracks of 2″ and over. The name comes from the sound made by the bongs when knocked together.

Some bong-bongs have large holes drilled through the blade to reduce the weight of the piton. These bongs are called Lightening Bongs. Diagram p. 94.

Boots. Boots specifically designed for hill-walking, rock climbing and mountaineering. The design of boots varies greatly, depending on the ultimate use. Boots for hill-walking are usually simple and cheap, made from supple leather, with flexible soles and few refinements.

Rock climbing boots are of two types. There is the lightweight boot for the specialist rock climber (see *Kletterschuhe* and *P.A.*) used almost exclusively for outcrop climbing, and a more conventional boot used for rock climbing under more serious conditions, as in the Alps. The second type of boot will have close fitting uppers, narrow welts and stiffened soles, to make better use of small footholds and to give the foot support.

Mountaineering boots, for all round use on rock and ice, are of a generally heavier construction and will have most of the following features—one-piece upper of good quality leather, multiple leather soles, narrow welts, stiffened soles, sewn-in or multiple tongues, hinged heel, built-in short leather stoptout and some system of hooks for lacing. The most modern design of boots have a rubber flap covering and protecting the lacing system.

For winter and high altitude climbing, double boots are made. The outer boots are normal mountain boots, the inner boots are usually thick felt with some light leather for reinforcement on the sole and ankle.

Almost all boots made nowadays have composition rubber soles with a special cleated pattern, but some people still use the old fashioned nailed boots (see *Nails* and *Vibrams*). Diagram p. 288.

Bottoming. A piton is said to bottom, if it reaches the back of a crack before it is fully inserted; such a crack is called a bottoming crack. (See *Blind Crack* and *Tie-off*.)

Bouldering. The practice of climbing on boulders—a common pastime among all climbers. Suitable boulders are found in every mountain district and in some low hill districts. Boulder climbing is usually of a very high standard, since a fall is rarely serious.

Bowline Knot. One of the original knots used to tie one end of a climbing rope round the waist of a

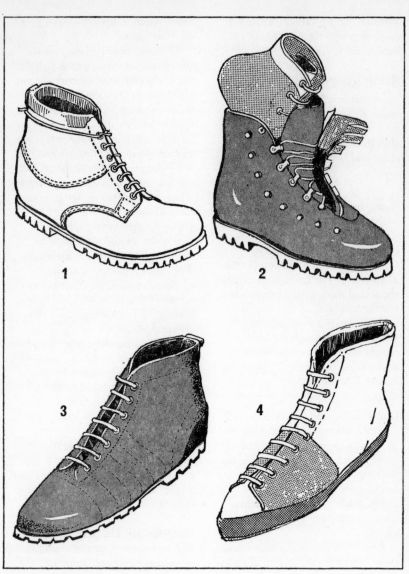

Boots. (1) *Hill-walking boot*
(2) *Double Mountain boot* (3) *Kletterschuhe*
(4) *P.A. rockclimbing boot.*

climber. With the advent of waist-
lines, harnesses and the like,
climbing ropes are not often tied
round the waist nowadays and the
bowline has been superceeded for
this purpose by the Fisherman's
Knot and the Tarbuk Knot. Never-
theless, the bowline can be used for
a variety of purposes and is one of
the most useful knots in
mountaineering. Diagram p. 78.

Bowline on the Bight. A knot
which is suitable for a climber
tying himself in the middle of a
climbing rope. Not often used as
the overhand knot is much easier
to remember and use.

Box Quilting. A technique used in
the manufacture of duvet equipment to eliminate the cold spots
formed at the seams in normal
quilting. A narrow strip of material
is sewn between the walls, to give
a box effect—the down holding the
walls apart and providing insulation
at the seams. The same effect is
sometimes produced by making the
duvet in two sections of normal
quilting, with lightweight muslin
as the inner walls and with the seams
of each section not corresponding.
This is more effective, but more
expensive to manufacture and is
only used in the highest quality
equipment. Diagram p. 46.

Brake Bar. A short thick metal bar,
designed to fit on a karabiner and
intended for use as a friction device
for abseiling and rescue work.
Although brake bars are light and
easy to carry, they are not as effective
as other devices and are rarely used
in earnest.

Braking. The act of arresting a fall
on a steep snow slope by using an
ice-axe as a brake. The recognized
method is for the falling climber to
turn over on his stomach, head
pointing up the slope and feet
down, though this position may be
difficult to achieve in a few seconds
if the climber is rolling down the
slope; then, as soon as possible, to
drive the pick of his ice-axe gradually into the slope, setting up a
brake which will eventually bring
the fall to a halt. The axe should be
held with one hand on the shaft and
the other hand firmly around the
head, to prevent the axe being
snatched away by the force of the
braking procedure.

A fall, with possibly serious consequences, can always be averted on
steep snow providing the climber
acts quickly and applies this breaking
procedure effectively. If a fall pulls
down other members of a roped
party moving together on snow,
each member should brake with his
ice-axe. It is, however, most unusual
for one falling climber, roped to
others, to pull the remainder of the
party down as such falls can be
quickly checked with the rope and
an ice-axe driven quickly into the
slope by one or all the stable
members of the party. (See *Glissade*.)
Diagram p. 113.

Braking is also used to describe
the action of braking the rope when
a dynamic belay is being used to
hold a falling leader. (See *Dynamic
Belay*.)

Brèche. (*French*.) Strictly a col, but
used more specifically in the French
Alps to describe a high gap on a
ridge which is usually small and
narrow, and enclosed by steep walls.

Chimney climbing. (1) Bridging
(2) Back and foot.

Bridging. A method of climbing chimneys and corners; it can also be any series of upward movements on a rock face when the legs are astride and the feet are being used on pressure holds. In chimneys, suitable footholds and handholds on each wall must be available, and upward progress is made by placing one foot and one hand on each wall and pressing downwards and outwards against the walls. Basically the same method is used to climb corners by bridging, but because of the more open angle of the walls, more positive holds are needed to maintain balance, unless the rock is very rough and friction can be used.

The technique of bridging can in fact be used on most types of rock formation and is particularly suitable for climbing overhanging and loose rocks. Correctly used, the technique is not strenuous and puts less strain on loose holds than more conventional techniques. Diagram p. 30.

British Mountaineering Council. A body which represents British climbing clubs and acts as a spokesman in the wider interests of British mountaineering. The Council, founded in 1944, has made considerable strides to ensure the improvement of mountaineering equipment by insisting that manufacturers should guarantee their products under specifications laid down by the Council—specifications formulated after exhaustive tests had been carried out on defective or weak equipment by members of special sub-committees set up for this purpose.

Brocken Spectre. The unusual phenomenon of seeing ones own shadow cast on a bank of cloud or mist. The Brocken is a peak in the Harz Mountains where the spectre may have been first seen.

Bucket Step. A very large step cut in snow or ice. Used to change direction in a zig-zag ascent, for resting, or to make the ascent of a slope easier if it is being used often (e.g. by porters on a Himalayan climb).

Bugaboo. A special type of offset piton (q.v.) which has a long thin blade.

Bulge. A rounded overhang. The word is normally only used for small overhangs of this type, where the climber would be out of balance for only a few moves. Sometimes, however, it is used to describe a large section of a face or a ridge.

Buttress. A part of a cliff or a mountain standing proud from the rest and usually defined by a gully on either side. A buttress can be a small feature, only a few feet across and giving only one climb, or it can be a very large feature with several subsidiary grooves and arete, all of which may give climbs. In the Alps, buttress is used of features which might equally well be called a spur. The crest of a buttress is often a ridge.

Cacolet. (*French*.) A carrying frame made of canvas and straps worn like a rucsac in which an injured climber can sit.

C.A.F. *Club Alpin Francais*—French Alpine Club, founded in 1874. In the history of mountaineering the C.A.F. has been one of the most influential bodies on the international scene, responsible for major innovations which have changed the course of the pastime. Headquarters in Paris; publishes a glossy magazine, *La Montagne,* issued five times a year. The club is indirectly state-aided through the Féderation Française de la Montagne (see *F.F.M.*) and has a full-time secretariat and offices in Chamonix-Mont Blanc and at La Berarde in the Dauphiné. The administration is deployed regionally in nine sections throughout France, each of which has its own publications. There is also a section in Algeria.

Cagoule. (*French.*) A type of anorak, made in lightweight waterproof material, which comes below the knees, intended for use on bivouacs in conjunction with a Pied d'Elephant (q.v.).

C.A.I. *Club Alpino Italiano*—Italian Alpine Club, founded in 1863, is divided into regional sections, with a total membership of over 100,000. There are offices at Milan, Turin and Aosta. Publishes a monthly journal, *Revista Mensile.*

C.A.S. *Club Alpin Suisse*—Swiss Alpine Club, founded in 1863, probably the most conservative, efficient and businesslike organisation of its type in the world. Headquarters at Zurich, with full-time administration; publishes simultaneously a monthly information magazine and a quarterly feature article magazine both called *Die Alpen* (*Les Alpes*). The club also produces books of a specialised and more general interest in three languages. The organisation is divided into several regional sections, which are virtually autonomous and each has its meeting rooms in towns and cities. There is an association of British members, based in London.

Caire. (*French.*) A secondary rock peak or a large gendarme in the Maritime Alps, France.

Cairn. A pile of stones erected to mark a summit, a spot height, a pass, etc. Cairns are also put up at intervals along some mountain paths to mark the way in misty weather. A small cairn is sometimes built at the foot of a rock climb, to indicate where it starts.

Cale. (*French.*) A small piece of wood used to block a wide shallow hole, so that a piton can be hammered into it. The technique is very effective and is used mainly on limestone.

Calotte. (*French.*) A crest, tip, or pyramid of snow which caps the summit of a mountain. The name is used for several summits in the Mont Blanc chain, in the Dauphiné and in the Valais Alps.

Cambridge Belay. An old fashioned name for a direct belay.

Camp. A stage in the climbing of high mountains in the Andes, Himalayas, etc. Camps are set up from the foot of a mountain, the first one being called base camp and the second sometimes advanced base camp. The number of camps set up to climb a mountain depends on the distance the climbers can cover each day, allowing time for transport of food and equipment, for the weather and technical difficulties. As many as eight or nine camps may be necessary before the summit can be reached.

Cannelures. (*French.*) Literally flutings. The word is used mainly in the Mont Blanc region to describe the parallel shallow U-shaped channels which occur frequently on Chamonix granite. These channels usually provide finger-jams and side-pulls and are sometimes large enough for hand-jams.

Cannon Stone. A finger of rock protruding from a crack or chimney, or a finger of rock at the base of a cliff which often serves to indicate the start of a climb. The name is usually only applied to well known features.

Capstone. A large, flat chockstone in a chimney or gully, often closing the exit and which forms some kind of overhang or even a small cave.

C.C. Climbers' Club, one of the two largest domestic clubs in Britain, founded in 1898. The original membership was drawn from London and the Oxford and Cambridge Universities and so the activities of the club have always been concentrated around North Wales and the southern parts of England, for which it publishes a series of guidebooks. Publishes an annual journal and an annual information bulletin, *New Climbs.* Owns several huts, in North Wales, Derbyshire and Cornwall.

Chain. A mountain system consisting of a collection of more or less parallel ranges, and possibly including plateaux.

Chalk. A soft, grey-white coloured rock composed largely of calcium carbonate, which is highly unsuitable for climbing. Chalk is so soft that it has been used as practice for cutting steps in ice!

Channel Piton. A piton made in an angular U-shape, of various lengths and widths, designed for use in wide cracks. The eye of a channel piton, is usually in one side of the channel, specially enlarged for the purpose. Diagram p. 94.

Cheating. A colloquial expression, sometimes used in a humorous sense, to describe climbing which is accepted as 'free' in principle, but in fact needs a number of artificial aids and sometimes sophisticated protection techniques.

Chest Tie. A method of roping up, preferred by Continental climbers, where the rope is tied around the chest and shoulders, instead of the waist.

Chimney. A fissure in a rock face which will admit the body. Many types of chimneys are encountered in rock climbing, from clean-cut splits in a rock face, to wide cracks in corners. The technique used to climb a chimney depends on its width and the number and quality of holds available. (See *Back and Foot, Back and Knee* and *Bridging.*) Diagram p. 30.

Chockstone. A stone or boulder

wedged in a crack, a chimney or a gully. In cracks and chimneys these stones are useful as handholds, footholds, running belays and some-times stances. Chockstones in chimneys and gullies may be difficult to surmount and they often form cave pitches. A very large chockstone in a gully is sometimes called a jammed boulder, and they can often be avoided by a through route (q.v.). (See *Inserted Chockstone* and *Nuts*.)

Chockstoning. A method of climbing a steep thin crack by inserting a series of chockstones and standing in slings from them. Chockstoning is usually only carried out for short stretches of a climb, but there are one or two examples of climbs which rely almost entirely on this technique.

Chrome-molly. A colloquial name for the American type pitons, which are made from chrome-molybdenum steel.

Cima, Cimon. (*Italian.*) A mountain with steep sides and a rounded summit. The name is used mainly in the Dolomites.

Cime. (*French.*) The summit of a secondary peak. In conversation, it may mean the summit of any mountain.

Cirque. (*French.*) A deep rounded hollow with steep sides at the head of a valley, formed through erosion by snow and ice, and thus character-istic of regions which have been glaciated. In regions which still have glaciers, cirques can often be seen, filled with névé which feeds the

glacier below. In regions where glaciation took place in the past, cirques are often filled with small lakes, damned with moraine or a rock wall. Mountains in heavily glaciated regions may have several adjoining cirques, separated by sharp arêtes formed by the erosion of the walls between the cirques. The back wall of a cirque is often a steep crag suitable for rock climbing. Diagram p. 37.

Cisalp. *Centre Internationale de Secours Alpins.* This is a telephone service which was started by the U.I.A.A. and is effective in France, Switzerland, Italy, Germany, Austria and Jugoslavia. The centre is located at Geneva, where all the addresses and telephone numbers of mountain rescue posts are available for these countries. To make en-quiries about a missing person, one telephones Geneva 11, asks for Cisalp, and states where the person is climbing. Cisalp then supplies the addresses and telephone numbers of rescue posts in the vicinity and it is up to the inquirer to contact these posts himself. If he is successful in establishing the whereabouts of the missing person, he can give instructions for a search or rescue to be organized. Payment for all telephone calls and rescue services must be met by the inquirer.

Clapier. (*French.*) An area of large blocks resting on a flat or easy angled slope. The term is used mainly in the Maritime Alps, France.

Classic Routes. Ways up mountains which are routes of character, of historic interest, of great difficulty, of popularity or a combination of any of these features. Routes are designated as classic only many years after the first ascent; the features which place them in this category are hard to define. Difficult routes achieved early in the exploration of mountains always become classic, e.g. the Old Brenva route on Mont Blanc; rock climbs and snow and ice climbs which offer fine climbing of no great difficulty, in impressive surroundings and with good views frequently become classic, e.g. the Mer de Glace face of the Grépon, Chamonix, and the Biancograt of the Piz Bernina, St. Moritz; routes of average difficulty which are consistently followed by parties sometimes become classic, e.g. the Schalligrat of the Weisshorn, Zermatt; difficult routes of outstanding merit and length which may be frequented by expert mountaineers may be called classic, e.g. the North Face of the Piz Badile. The definitions may be pursued in this manner indefinitely.

In Britain, some rock climbs are said to be classic, more or less for the same reasons outlined above, though there may be many more climbs of equal merit which are not given this designation. A classic route on a British crag is often the most interesting and most typical route on the crag, and as such is probably the best climb for a party to do who are on a short visit.

Cliff. A smooth steep face of rock. (See *Crag.*)

Climber. A person who climbs routes on mountains which require the use of ropes and other items of mountaineering equipment. The distinction is made with walker, meaning 'hill-walker', a person who climbs mountains by walking routes and therefore has no need of mountaineering equipment. (See *Walker.*)

Climbing Irons. The only equivalent in English for crampons. The name is no longer used. (See *Crampons.*)

Clinker Nails. Climbing nails made from soft iron, and fitted to the edge of soles and heels of nailed climbing boots. The nails have good friction properties on rock. The fitting consists of driving the spikes of the nails through the welts from the boot sole, and turning them over the edge of the welts. (See *Nails.*) Diagram p. 85.

Clinometer. An instrument for measuring the dip of strata and angle of a slope—a useful novelty in mountaineering to disprove exaggerations about the steepness of snow and ice slopes. A hand clinometer can be carried conveniently in a pocket and weighs less than half a pound. The principal is a weighted disc and gravity. The angle of a slope is read off in degrees marked on the disc through a prisim, and holds good for angles of elevation and depression.

Clocher. (*French.*) A rock peak with steep sides and a rounded summit. The diminuitive of Clocher, Clocheton, is frequently used for small groups of peaks of this type.

Cnoc. (*Gaelic.*) A knock or hill. It is from this word that the modern

'Knock' is derived. Used mainly in Ireland.

Coiling. The methods of coiling a rope so that it can be easily carried. There are several methods of coiling, all of which are equally effective. The method generally used by British climbers is to loop the rope into coils about three feet long, finishing with a special knot similar to whipping, so that the coiled rope can be carried around the shoulders. A certain amount of skill is needed to coil a rope without kinking it badly.

Col. (*French*.) A pass. This can vary from a road pass, to a pass high in the mountains. The name is often used for a major gap in a ridge, which may or may not be used as a means of access from one valley to another. Diagram p. 57.

Combe, Coomb, Coombe. A short, narrow valley, similar in some cases to a cirque, but with more gentle sides and grass covered slopes. The name is used frequently in the Lake District and in the West Country.

Combined Tactics. The assistance given to a leader by other members of a roped party to overcome a difficult pitch. The leader stands on the shoulders or head of one or more members of the party, so that holds more than ten feet above the stance can be reached. Every safeguard is given to the leader during such manoeuvres, and assisting members of the party are properly belayed. This practice is not usually classified as artificial climbing.

Continuous. A term used to describe an unbroken rock climb as distinct from the many climbs which have scrambles over grass and vegetation between pitches. The term is sometimes used to indicate that a climb is of continuous and sustained difficulty.

Contour. An imaginary line on the ground drawn on a map to join up all points of equal height above sea-level. In this way the shape and steepness of the land can be accurately represented. In Britain, the Ordnance Survey one-inch maps give contours at every increase of 50 feet in elevation. Maps of the Alps, scale 1:50,000, have a contour interval of 20 metres. The ground between contour lines at different levels on some large scale maps is tinted with different colours to enable the reader to follow the map more easily.

Contouring is also used to describe the practice of walking across a hillside or round a mountain at the same height (i.e. following the imaginary contour). This is often done when one wishes to reach a point on the other side of a slope or mountain without gaining or losing any uneccessary height. Diagram p. 37.

Cordée. (*French*.) A party of roped climbers.

Cordillera. A collection or parallel or connected mountain ranges. The name is mainly used in the Americas and particularly in the Andes, where all the major ranges are called Cordillera.

Corner. A place on a cliff where two walls meet more or less at right-

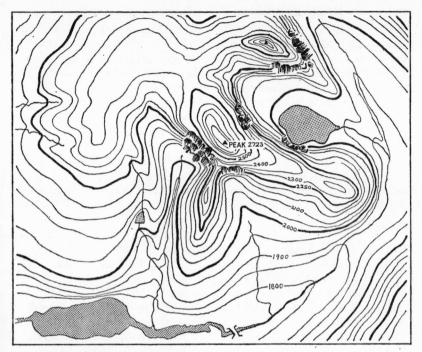

A contour map, with spot height. The feature to the NWW of the Peak is a typical cirque, with a dammed lake and steep back wall.

angles. The name is nearly always applied to inside corners (as in the room of a house), but is sometimes used to describe a vertical arête of this type. Such a feature is a very common pitch in rock climbing. If a crack is present, a corner may be climbed by jamming or laybacking. If no crack is present, a corner may be climbed on one wall, or by bridging. On the whole, bridging is the best and least strenuous technique for corners. Corners are usually steep and sometimes over-hanging.

Cornice. An overhanging lip of snow raised along the crest of a ridge; this is caused by the prevailing wind building up fresh snow to an inclined bank, the leeward side of which will eventually form a lip. There are many cornices on ridges in the Alps, and they occur frequently on any snow mountain. Cornices must be avoided at all costs as they are liable to collapse under the weight of a person. Some ridges have double cornices which overhang each side of the ridge alternately. When a cornice breaks off, it may break much further back than the crest of the ridge and so the safest line to follow is well below the crest of the ridge, on the side away from the cornice.

Cornices often block the exit from couloirs. If there is no easy way round the cornice, it may be necessary to chop part of it away, or even tunnel through it, to reach the ridge above. Diagram p. 39.

Couloir. (*French*.) A gully in the Alps and other high mountain ranges. Most couloirs are at least partly snow filled and a bergschrund often guards the entrance. Couloirs are natural channels for avalanches and stone falls, which may come from the snow in the couloir itself, from the cornice which may close the couloir or from the surrounding walls. In a snow couloir, the avalanche tracks are often clearly visible and an avalanche cone may fill the bergschrund. The danger of stone falls and avalanches can only be avoided at certain times of the day and year, as early in the morning after a hard frost in summer and when the couloir is in shadow in winter. When stones are falling, the best route is well over to one side, preferably under an impending wall.

Rock couloirs in the Alps are unlike British gullies; they are usually more open and steep, with fewer chockstones and level intervals of scree. Narrow rock couloirs are sometimes called *couloir-cheminées*.

In guide books, the description of the ascent of couloirs often refers to the *true* left and right banks (i.e. as looking in descent)—this sometimes causes confusion and care must be taken to ensure which method of description is being used. This is usually stated in the introduction to the guide book.

Coupled Pitons. A method of driving two pitons together into a crack wider than any piton the climber has available at the time. Coupled pitons tend to be less secure than a single piton, but they can be adequate for direct aid. Pitons of most types can be coupled by inserting the pitons with the backs of the blades touching. It is usual to tie-off (q.v.) coupled pitons. Diagram p. 118.

A snow ridge with a cornice.

Cow's Tail. A device used in artificial climbing, so that a climber can temporarily link himself to a piton and dispense with the need for tension from the rope. A cow's tail can be simply made from a short loop of rope and a karabiner, but the best type is made from one or two fiffi hooks tied onto a loop of line, giving both versatility and ease of use.

Crack. A fissure in a rock face which, at its widest, will admit no more than one arm, one leg, or both; one of the most common types of rock problems in all degrees of difficulty. The techniques of climbing cracks are all muscular and depend on the width of the crack. Wide cracks are usually climbed by wedging, hand-jamming and foot-jamming. Narrow cracks are usually climbed by finger and toe jamming and sometimes by layback. Although crack climbing tends to be more strenuous than other types, it is usually very safe since cracks offer good possibilities for protection by thread belays and chockstones. (See *Foot-jam, Hand-jam, Finger-jam, Toe-jam, Wedging* and *Layback*.)

Crack-tack. An alternative name for the Rurp piton (q.v.).

Crag. A steep, rugged and sometimes broken rock face (see *Cliff*).

Crag-fast. Stranded and unable to move on a cliff. The term does not apply to climbers, but to sheep and goats which become crag-fast in search of fresh grass. Many of these animals are rescued by climbers, who should be belayed and use a rope. The animals often panic when approached, and fall over the cliff, so it is far better to wait a few days till the animal is too weak from hunger to move violently, before attempting a rescue.

Crampons. (*French*.) Forged strips of steel fitted with spikes which are strapped to the soles of climbing boots for climbing on snow and ice. Crampons are used to climb slopes of hard snow and ice slopes which might otherwise require step cutting and thus save a great deal of valuable time. There are two types of crampon, with 10 and 12 points. The 12 point crampons, sometimes called Lobster Claw Crampons, have the two extra points protruding forward at an angle from the toe end and are used for climbing very steep snow and ice (see *Front-pointing*). When wearing crampons, the climber should always walk flat-footed so that the spikes bite the slope simultaneously. This means that the angle of slopes which can be climbed in crampons (excluding front-pointing) is limited by the degree of flexibility of the climbers ankles, as well as his nerve. Crampons can be useful on verglassed rock and on some mixed routes, it is better to climb the easier rock sections in crampons to save continually taking them off and putting them on again. Many types of crampon straps are available, but the best are in nylon, with quick release buckles and with a separate strap for the heel and front of the foot. Some types of crampons are adjustable, to save having to buy a new pair with each new pair of boots. For long and difficult ice climbs, it is advisable to have crampons with tungsten tips, which retain their sharpness longer than normal crampons. (See *Balling Up and Nails*.) Diagram p. 70.

Crête. (*French*.) A narrow, jagged ridge. It is a pitch or section of a route, rather than a whole ridge of a mountain. It can also be a rib.

Crevasse. A split in the surface of the glacier, caused by the changing course of a glacier or by a change in the angle of the slope over which the glacier flows. The changing course of a glacier causes marginal crevasses (i.e. splits at the edges), and curved longitudinal crevasses in mid-stream; the changing angle of slope over which the glacier flows causes marginal crevasses and transverse crevasses in mid-stream. Crevasses are said to be (1) open, when they are visible and can be avoided; (2) bridged, when they are visible and partly spanned by snow or ice which may afford a way across; (3) closed, when they are not visible, but can be identified by a crack or hollow in the surface of the glacier; (4) hidden, when they are invisible below a covering of snow. The last condition is dangerous, and parties crossing a glacier with hidden crevasses should rope up and proceed cautiously. The upper part of the glacier, where the névé lies, can be most troublesome in this respect. (See *Bergschrund, Crevasse Rescue* and *Glacier*.) Diagram p. 57.

Crevasse Bridging Equipment
Equipment for making a temporary bridge across a crevasse. Portable ladders and poles are used by high altitude expeditions to expediate the porterage of provisions and equipment to higher camps.

Crevasse Rescue. The method and operation for the rescue of persons from crevasses. There are numerous ways; the best are only possible when the fallen climber has prusik loops or some device (q.v.) attached to the climbing rope, and when there are at least two other members in the party with a spare rope. The active rope attached to the climber must first of all be secured to prevent a further slip down the crevasse; this can be done with an ice-axe, but another member of the party will be required to hold the rope if the axe cannot be buried deep enough in the glacier. The fallen climber, if uninjured, should then be able to ascend the fixed rope with the aid of prusik loops to a point a foot or two below the top of the crevasse. The rope will probably have become embedded in the lip of the crevasse, unless it is very hard snow, and the last movements over the edge are best assisted by another climber using the spare rope, possibly from the other side of the crevasse. An alternative method is for the climber to stand in prusik slings, one on each rope, and to raise each leg alternately while the ropes are pulled from above. Crevasse rescue can be very difficult when there are only two climbers, or when the fallen climber is injured. It is very exhausting when no prusik loops or prusik devices are attached to the rope. (See *Prusik*.)

Croda. (*Italian*.) In the Dolomites, a rock ridge or peak.

Crusted Snow. Snow whose surface has been compacted to form a hard crust, either by melting and freezing, or by wind pressure, or both.

Crusted snow may be good for walking over early in the day, but when the crust is not strong enough to support a climbers weight, it can be very tiring to walk on, especially on large level snowfields. The condition is very common—firm in the morning, brittle in the afternoon. On steep slopes the surface beneath the crusted snow should be examined for ice, as this combination can be dangerous. (See *Wind-slab*.)

Crux. The most difficult move or pitch on a rock climb or mountaineering route, and usually indicated as such in the guide book description.

Cwm. (*Welsh.*) A cirque (q.v.). Although the U.I.A.A. has designated cwm as the international word for the feature, its use is still limited and nearly all climbers use their native word.

Delicate. Attributed in rock climbing to a move or pitch which requires balance, a light touch and good technique; the opposite of forceful and strenuous climbing. Walls, slabs and grooves give much delicate climbing. Friction is often an important factor in the climbing of difficult and delicate routes.

Dénivellation. (*French.*) The vertical interval between two known heights. The word is generally used to indicate the vertical height of serious climbing on a mountaineering route.

Dent. (*French.*) Literally a tooth. Often applied to steep mountains with rounded summits, in the French Alps.

Depegged. A colloquial term to describe an artificial route which normally has all its pitons left in place, but which, for some reason or other (usually pecuniary) has had the pitons removed.

Dépittoneur. (*French.*) A term generally used by the French to describe a gadget for extracting pitons. This usually takes the form of a metal bar and a short length of chain. The chain is linked to the piton with a karabiner and the metal bar hammered, so that the extracting force is directly in line with the piton.

Descendeur. (*French.*) A friction gadget for abseiling. The general principal is a piece of aluminium alloy specially shaped, so that the rope can be wrapped round it in a particular way, to create the friction necessary for a controlled descent. The advantages of a descendeur lie mainly in the fact that the abseil rope does not come into contact with the body, making abseiling faster and less painful. The main disadvantage of most types of descendeur is that they kink the rope, and therefore must be used very carefully. The original descendeur was made by Pierre Allain of Paris, but many other types now exist, of which the figure-of-8 is undoubtedly the best. (See *Abseil* and *Figure-of-8*.) Diagram p. 13.

Diagonal Cutting. Cutting a line of steps in snow and ice in a diagonal direction across a slope. With the advent of modern snow and ice

techniques, diagonal cutting is
rarely used except for traversing a
slope or descending.

Direct. A direct way up part of a
cliff, where more circuitous routes
exist. Direct routes tend to be more
difficult than ordinary routes
because they follow steeper rocks.
Sometimes an artificial direct route
is forced, because the idea of a
direct route may be aesthetically
pleasing (see *Direttissima*). There are
also direct starts and direct finishes
to many climbs which start and
finish in a relatively easy manner.

Direct Belay. A makeshift type of
belay, used mainly in the Alps and
particularly when a party is moving
together on easy ground and a short
section of difficulty is encountered,
requiring some kind of temporary
belay. The active rope is passed over
a knob of rock, or through a karabiner
on a sling, attached to a spike or
piton. The other members of the
party are not usually belayed in the
accepted sense, as the idea of the
direct belay is to save time.
Although a direct belay may give
some psychological support to the
party, it is not likely to be very
effective for holding a fallen leader
and should be used very carefully.

Direttissima. (*Italian.*) A route
which follows a direct line from the
foot of a face to the summit of a
mountain. The name is used mainly
in the Dolomites, where the cult of
the Direttissima was born. In recent
years many such routes in the
Dolomites have been forced with
the all out use of artificial climbing
and unlimited use of expansion
bolts. With the constant search for

new routes and new forms of
mountaineering the *idea* of the
direttissima has spread to other
centres in the Alps and even further
afield.

Distress Signal. A signal intended
to attract attention in the event of an
accident. It consists of six blasts of a
whistle, or torch flashes, or shouts
in a minute, followed by a minute's
silence and thus repeated until there
is an acknowledgement. The
replying signal is in the same form,
but with three blasts, flashes or
shouts in a minute. The use of
whistles, torches and shouting in
mountain districts should be carefully controlled, in case they are
mistaken for a distress signal.

Modern distress signals, in the
form of portable hand-flares are now
available, but as yet very few
climbers or walkers seem to carry
them.

Divide. A watershed, the high
country separating two river
systems or basins. Sometimes used
as the name of a range of mountains.

D.Ö.A.V. *Deutscher Oesterreichischer
Alpen Verein*—Austro-German
Alpine Federation, founded in 1873.
After several separations and
reunifications, the best known
unification being that of 1929, the
clubs are again separate.

Dodero Test. The U.I.A.A.
standard for climbing ropes, which
consists of a drop test, named in
honour of Professor Dodero on
whose work it is based. The details
of the test are fairly simple. A length
of rope is fixed at one end, passed
through a hole in a steel plate which

represents the curve of a karabiner, and an 80 kg. weight is fastened to the other end. The angles of the ropes and the various distances are all controlled carefully. The rope must withstand two drops without failing and the maximum force generated in the rope must not exceed 1200 kg. This is the standard for ropes to be used singly (i.e. Extra Full-weight hawser-laid rope and 11 mm. kernmantel rope). The standard for ropes to be used double has a weight of 40 kg. and the force generated must not exceed 600 kg. Other sections of the test cover extensibility, stability, weight, material, construction and finish. Ropes which come up to the standard of the Dodero test carry the distinctive U.I.A.A. label.

Dolerite. An igneous rock forming minor intrusions, more coarse grained than basalt, which it otherwise resembles. Dolerite is often very shattered and can be the source of loose rocks or can be the cause of the formation of an over-hang of more compact rocks, through differential erosion.

Dolomite. A magnesium limestone, varying in colour from grey to dark red, found predominantly in the eastern Alps in a region enclosed by the Adige, Puster and Piave valleys, formerly called the Venetian Alps or South Tyrol. The Dolomites are a remarkable series of summits, mostly around the 9,000 foot level, with a tremendous collection of vertical faces and ridges. It is one of the most popular rock climbing areas in the Alps.

Dôme. (*French.*) A rounded summit

which is often the head of a snow-field or ice-field.

Dore. (*Cumbrian.*) A gap between walls of rock which is not unlike a brèche. The name is used almost exclusively in the Lake District.

Double Fisherman's Knot. A Fisherman's knot (q.v.) with a half-hitch tied into each half of the knot. This is very secure and is frequently used by climbers for joining slings and abseil ropes.

Dry Glacier. A glacier of bare ice. The lower sections of many glaciers are dry in summer as the snow covering melts off completely. All the crevasses on a dry glacier are clearly visible, so it is not usual for a party to rope up.

Dubbin. A waterproof grease for preserving the leather of boots.

Dülfer. A prominent Austrian mountaineer who made many important ascents in the Eastern Alps in the early 1900's. His name is used by continental mountaineers to describe certain rock climbing techniques. The Germans use Dülfer for a tension traverse, the French and Italians use Dülfer for a layback. There is also a Dülfer abseil, which is a modification of the classic method of abseiling.

Duvet. (*French.*) Literally down. The name adopted by all climbers for a jacket made from lightweight cloth, filled with down. Duvet jackets are light and roll up into a small space and are therefore ideal for carrying on long climbs to provide warmth in cold weather and on bivouacs.

Many other duvet articles are made for climbing, such as duvet vests, duvet gloves, duvet trousers and duvet socks. (See *Pied d'Elephant*, *Sleeping Bag* and *Box Quilting*.) Diagram p. 46.

Dynamic Belay. A method of stopping the progress of a falling leader by the application of a gradual force on the climbing rope, by the second man. The force created by a falling leader may be enough to pull the second man from his stance, thus rendering him less likely to hold the fall, and may even be enough to break the rope under certain conditions. The principle of the dynamic belay is to absorb the force of the fall gradually, by allowing the rope to run, under friction, around the waist and then to gradually apply an increasing force on the moving rope with gloved hands to eventually stop the fall. It is only possible to apply a dynamic belay when the second man is firmly belayed and is standing in the correct position, using a waist belay. Gloves are essential to prevent damage to the second's hands. Unless the belayer is practised in using the dynamic belay it is quite possible that he may allow the leader to fall the full length of the rope, with the possibility of a heavy jerk coming directly onto the belay and extra damage to the leader falling the extra distance, so it is probably better to apply a very good stopping belay and rely on the elastic proper-ties of the nylon rope to absorb the shock of the fall. With modern nylon ropes, cases of ropes breaking are rare, unless the rope catches on some sharp projection. If a dynamic belay is used with nylon rope, care is required to prevent too much friction on the rope, especially against another piece of nylon, as it is liable to melt.

Dynamic Posture. A very particular crouch position of the body in walking and climbing which enhances balance and conserves energy. In walking, it is the easy roll of the hips timed carefully with deliberate and accurate placing of the feet on the ground ahead. Leg strides are even and unhurried; the arms are limp and hands free from pockets, but able to steady the body on rocky passages across rough terrain; the trunk of the body is leant forward in balance with the steepness of the slope ahead; the eyes are focussed on the ground only a few feet away. In climbing, dynamic posture is more difficult to define, especially since it is impossible to achieve on certain types of rock problem such as cracks and chimneys. It may be said to be a constant state of balance and the correct application of technique to overcome rock problems in the easiest and least strenuous manner. Dynamic posture is very difficult to aquire, except by long practice.

Èboulement. (*French.*) Strictly the word éboulement is used by the French to describe the scar left on a mountainside or cliff face, which is formed by a large rock fall. The scar is usually a lighter colour than the rest of the face, because of the unweathered rocks which have been exposed, and the rock in the scar region is invariably very brittle and loose. Éboulement is also used in a

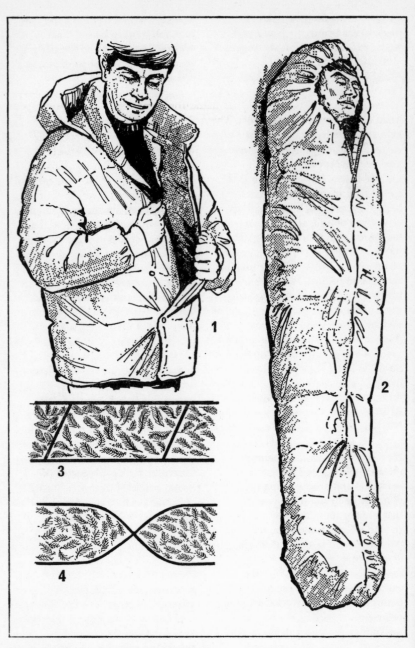

Duvet equipment (1) *Duvet Jacket* (2) *Sleeping Bag*
(3) *Box-quilting* (4) *Normal quilting.*

colloquial sense to describe the rock fall or avalanche causing the scar.

Edge. Sometimes used to describe a sharp vertical arête of rock. Also appears frequently in the names of Gritstone outcrops in the Pennines; e.g. Stanage Edge, Frogatt Edge, Gardom's Edge etc.

Eight-thousander. A colloquial name for a mountain of greater altitude than 8,000 metres (26,247 feet). There are 14 known eight-thousanders (not counting their own subsidiary tops), all in the Himalaya and Karakoram ranges. All the peaks have been climbed, several more than once, including Mount Everest.

Mountain	*Height metres*	*feet*	*Year first climbed*	*Expedition*
Mount Everest	8,848	29,028	1953	British
K2* (Mount Godwin-Austen)	8,611	28,252	1954	Italian
Kanchenjunga	8,600	28,216	1955	British
Lhotse	8,511	27,923	1956	Swiss
Makalu	8,481	27,825	1955	French
Dhaulagiri	8,222	26,975	1960	Swiss
Cho Oyu	8,189	26,867	1954	Austrian
Mansalu	8,125	26,660	1956	Japanese
Nanga Parbat	8,125	26,660	1953	Austro-German
Annapurna I	8,078	26,504	1950	French
Gasherbrum I* (Hidden Peak)	8,068	26,470	1958	American
Broad Peak*	8,047	26,400	1957	Austrian
Gasherbrum II*	8,035	26,360	1956	Austrian
Shisha Pangma (Gosainthan)	8,013	26,291	1964	Chinese

* Situated in the Karakoram range.

Eliminate. A name sometimes given to British climbs which take an artificial line up a cliff, linking together pitches of a high standard.

En Flèche. (*French.*) A colloquial term sometimes used to describe a technique often used by guides with two clients on easy ground. The guide leads a pitch, then brings up the clients both at the same time, on separate ropes, one slightly behind the other.

Engineering. A colloquial name for complicated manoeuvres with ropes, methods of using aids in artificial climbing, special procedures for combining tactics, etc.

English 2000-footers. A list, compiled by W. T. Emslie, of the 348 summits in England which exceed the height of 2000 feet.

Escarpment. An inland cliff or steep slope, formed by the erosion of inclined strata of hard rocks. Consists frequently of a shorter, steeper slope known as the scarp face and a longer, more gradual slope known as the dip slope.

A typical escarpment, with a series of buttresses and gullies. The slope below the escarpment could be scree covered.

Many of the outcrops in Britain are escarpments. Diagram p. 48.

Espadrilles. (*French.*) Light, rope-soled boots once favoured by Continental climbers for difficult rock climbing. Espadrilles have now been largely superceeded by more sophisticated rock climbing boots (see *P.A.'s*), but are sometimes used because of their excellent gripping properties on wet greasy rock.

Étrier. (*French.*) A short lightweight ladder, consisting of two, three or four steps from 10 to 18 inches apart, used to assist the climbing of smooth or overhanging rocks by artificial means. Étriers are usually made either from alloy rungs fixed to a thin cord, or from a length of tape knotted or sewn in a special way to form loops for the feet. The étrier is attached to a piton by a karabiner. Sometimes a very short loop is provided at the top of the étrier, for use as a handhold. Normally each climber carries two or three étriers, which he uses alternately, but on very long artificial climbs the leader may carry enough étriers for a whole pitch. In the latter case the leader leaves an étrier on each piton to provide a continuous ladder for the second man, who recovers the étriers for the next pitch. (See *Artificial Climbing.*) Diagram p. 50.

Expanding Flake. A large flake of rock which is loose or partly detached and which moves when used by a climber. Expanding flakes usually give very hard pitches because they are difficult to protect properly. On artificial climbs, expanding flakes can be very

exciting because, as each piton is inserted, the flake expands more and all the previous pitons (including the one to which the climber is attached) tend to fall out!

Expansion Bolt. A device used in artificial climbing, and sometimes as a belay in free climbing when a rock face has no cracks into which a piton could be inserted. The climber drills a small hole (usually about $\frac{1}{4}''$ in diameter and $\frac{1}{2}''$ deep) into which he can fix the expansion bolt, which is then used in exactly the same way as a piton, for aid or security. The name comes originally from the expansion bolts used for building purposes, which consist of small leaves of steel with serrated sides through which a threaded bolt with a ringed head is screwed. When the bolt is screwed up, the leaves expand and grip the side of the crack. However, there are many devices now specially made for climbers and the name expansion bolt is still loosely applied to most of these, despite the fact that some of them use the principle of compression. The most effective type is a short, soft and square piece of metal, with an eye, which is slightly bigger than the hole drilled. When hammered into the hole, this type of bolt is compressed into the hole. Diagram p. 94.

Expedition. An organised party of mountaineers who set out to climb or explore in one of the more remote ranges of the world. Most expeditions have a definite objective, such as the ascent of an unclimbed mountain or a new route up a mountain, or the exploration and mapping of a small unknown area.

D

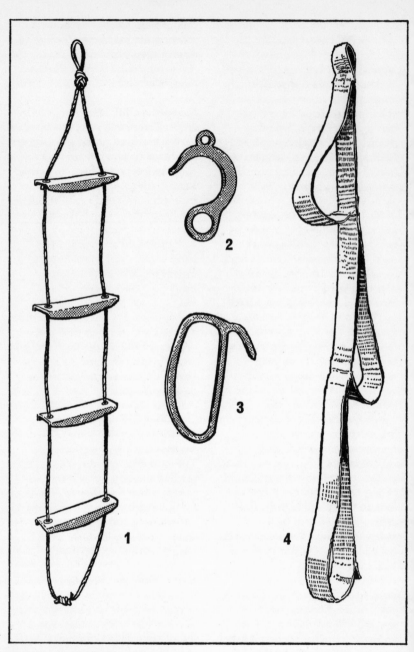

Étriers. (1) *Étrier made from cord and
alloy rungs* (2) *Fiffi hook* (3) *Griff-fiffi hook*
(4) *Étrier made from wide tape.*

An expedition includes the transport of provisions and equipment and the setting up of several camps (see *Approach March, Camp, Base Camp*).

Expeditions usually consist of at least six climbers, but this depends entirely on the area, the difficulty of the objective and the personal desires of the climbers involved. Large expeditions to the Himalayas often have a doctor and scientists, who wish to do research in their particular field, and as a consequence of the large number of personel, need large numbers of porters to transport the provisions and equipment. Most climbers prefer a smaller expedition, when the logistics of planning and carrying out the expedition are cut to a minimum.

Exposure. A climber's awareness or feeling of height; his appreciation of the open position on a steep cliff or mountain. This varies with individuals; some climbers may feel exposed in situations which are not exposed by the standards generally accepted. Some climbers are adversely affected by exposure; others enjoy it. Guide books usually indicate exposed pitches and routes.

The word exposure is also used to describe the serious effects which may result from exposure to climatic hazards. Phrases which are commonly used in this respect are 'suffering from exposure', 'risk of exposure' and 'death from exposure'. Exposure is not a strict medical term, but the essential feature of conditions described in this way is a reduced heat content of the body. This becomes serious when deep body temperature begins to fall, and can lead to death from hypothermia.

Extra Full-weight Rope. Nylon hawser-laid rope, also called No. 4, with a circumference of $1\frac{3}{8}''$, a breaking load of 4200 lbs. and a weight of $5\frac{1}{4}$ lbs. per 100 foot length. Extra full-weight rope is recommended for use singly as a climbing rope. Theoretically it is strong enough to withstand any fall, irrespective of the distance fallen by the leader, provided the rope does not catch on a sharp projection, etc.

Fell. (*Old Norse.*) A mountain; often used in the Lake District where it can denote either the side of a hill, a bulky spur or ridge or the name of a hill or mountain.

Fell-walking. Hill-walking (q.v.). The word is used especially in the North of England.

Fenêtre. (*French.*) A gap in a narrow ridge or a hole formed by a fallen stone, chockstone etc. Sometimes used as the name of a pass.

F.F.M. *Féderation Française de la Montagne.* In France, a national association, grant-aided by the government, whose objectives are to promote and sponsor mountaineering activities. Its staff are civil servants. This organisation is unique and it works closely with the C.A.F. (q.v.) and similar bodies. The work consists of raising funds for international expeditions, negotiating insurance schemes for mountaineers, administering registers of professional guides through regional bodies and arranging for improvements in the general welfare and facilities afforded to the French mountaineering community. Headquarters in Paris; publishes an annual report.

Fiffi. (*French.*) A small hook designed for permanent attachment to an étrier, instead of a karabiner. A long thin length of cord is joined from the climber's waist to a small hole in the top of the fiffi hook, so that when the climber has climbed past a piton, he can recover the étrier simply by pulling the cord, instead of having to climb back down. Some climbers use fiffi hooks without the recovery cord—partly because the cord complicates manoeuvres in artificial climbing and because a fiffi is easier and quicker to use than a karabiner. (See *Étrier, Griff-fiffi.*) Diagram p. 50.

Figure-of-8 Knot. A knot similar to the overhand knot, but with an extra turn which gives the knot a figure-of-8 shape. The advantage of the figure-of-8 knot is that it is much easier to untie than an overhand knot, particularly after some strain has been applied. Diagram p. 78.

Figure-of-8 Descendeur. An abseiling device made from thick wire or light alloy metal in a figure-of-8 shape. One of the holes is used to attach the device to the abseil harness with a karabiner; the other hole is used to pass the rope around to provide the friction for the descent. Most of the abseiling devices tend to kink the abseil rope badly; the design of the figure-of-8-descendeur reduces this tendency considerably. Diagram p. 13.

Finger-jam. The wedging of one or more fingers in a narrow crack to make a handhold. The technique can be applied in many ways, depending on the size of the crack and its shape. Finger-jamming in smooth cracks is very strenuous, as little lateral pressure can be applied by the fingers alone. A crack with a constriction can provide an excellent finger jam. In very shallow cracks where only the tips of the fingers can be inserted, a finger-jam can be made by inserting the first two fingers, one above the other. When the weight is applied the top finger wedges the lower finger into the crack. In general, finger-jams are less satisfactory than hand-jams (q.v.).

Fisherman's Knot. A knot for joining the ends of two ropes. The fisherman's knot is easy to tie and untie, is very secure and is used for a wide variety of purposes, such as joining abseil ropes and making a length of rope into a sling. Diagram p. 78.

Fish Plate. A colloquial name for a small piece of steel or alloy which is used to provide an attachment point to expansion bolts (q.v.) which do not have their own eye. The metal is drilled with two holes, one large and one small, and is bent at an angle of 45 or 90 degrees between the holes. The small hole can be fitted over the end of the bolt and secured with a nut and the large hole can be used to attach a karabiner. Fish plates vary in shape, size and design as they are almost all home made. Fish plates are sometimes called hangers. Diagram p. 94.

Fixed Rope or **Cable.** A thick rope and sometimes a wire cable, securely fixed over difficult pitches on some Alpine peaks e.g. the Matterhorn and the Dent du Géant. Fixed ropes are installed for various reasons, but usually only on popular routes used frequently by guides, partly to make the climb easier and faster for clients and also to provide some security in case of a descent in bad weather. The idea is regarded with mixed feelings in mountaineering circles.

Fixed ropes are also used by expeditions on long and difficult climbs, either to provide a handrail or support for porters carrying provisions and equipment, or to provide a quick means of climbing difficult stretches of the mountain which have previously been climbed by normal methods. In the latter case, the first party to climb a particular section of the mountain fixes ropes, which can be used subsequently by the rest of the team, who ascend by prusik techniques (q.v.). By using the fixed ropes, the party can then reascend and descend the route far quicker than by normal means. Ropes are usually fixed up to a point from where the summit can be reached in a reasonable number of days. The ropes are then removed in descent.

Flake. A thin flat piece of rock which is usually partly detached from the rock face. Secure flakes sometimes provide good belays and handholds; loose flakes may do so when used in a certain direction. Large flakes often form cracks which can be used for jamming, laybacking and hand-traversing. A crack formed by a flake is often called a flake-crack.

Föhn Wind. A warm, dry south

wind prevalent in Switzerland during the early spring and late autumn. This helps crops on the northern grasslands and clears the winter snow in spring. An early Föhn causes avalanches during the winter-sports season.

Foot-jam. The wedging of a foot in a crack. If the crack has constrictions, foot-jamming is a straightforward technique. In a smooth or wide crack, pressure must be exerted by turning the foot in the crack. Diagram p. 72.

Foot Stance. A very small rock stance, sometimes only two good footholds. When a foot stance is used, the belay should be good and very tight. It is usually better for the second man to lead through as changing over in the limited space may be awkward.

Form. The ability to climb comfortably at one's best without undue effort or fatigue. A climber who is 'on form' is always physically and psychologically fit, but the degree of fitness varies from climber to climber, depending on the attitude of the individual. To an experienced climber, the mental side is often more important than the physical side, and he can usually retain his form with little effort. For most climbers, the only way to keep 'on form' is constant practice and it can be difficult to achieve form after a long lay off from climbing.

Four-thousander. A colloquial name for a mountain more than 4,000 metres (13,123 feet) high in the Alps. There are about seventy-five, the first ten of which in order of altitude, are given in the table overleaf. The ascent of all the four-thousanders has been the ambition of many alpinists and has been realised by few.

Mountain	Height metres	feet
Mont Blanc (continued)	4,807	15,771
Mont Blanc de Courmayeur	4,748	15,577
Mont Maudit	4,465	14,650
Pic Luigi Amedeo	4,407	14,459
Dôme du Goûter	4,340	14,121
Mont Blanc du Tacul	4,248	13,937
2. Monte Rosa, Dufourspitze	4,634	15,304
Nordend	4,609	15,121
Zumsteinspitze	4,563	14,970
Signalkuppe	4,556	14,947
3. Mischabel, Dom	4,545	14,913
Täschhorn	4,491	14,734
Nadelhorn	4,327	14,196
Lenzspitze	4,294	14,078
4. Lyskamm	4,527	14,852
5. Weisshorn	4,505	14,780
6. Matterhorn	4,477	14,690
7. Dent Blanche	4,357	14,295
8. Grand Combin	4,314	14,154
9. Finsteraarhorn	4,274	14,022
10. Zwillinge, Castor	4,226	13,865

F.R.C.C. Fell and Rock Climbing Club of the English Lake District, one of the two largest domestic clubs in Britain, founded in 1906. The original aim of the Fell and Rock was to promote interest for climbing in the Lake District, but now it has a nation-wide membership and activities. Owns a number of huts in the Lake District, but like other British Clubs has no permanent headquarters. Publishes an annual journal and a series of guidebooks.

Free Abseil. An abseil over an overhang, where the body is hanging free in space. (See *Abseil.*)

Friction Climbing. Climbing which depends on the adherence of the feet and hands on smooth and sloping holds, by the exertion of pressure and the use of opposing forces.

Friction climbing needs confidence, particularly in the feet, and good technique. It is usually delicate, but can be strenuous on account of the nature of available handholds.

Friction Hitch. Another name for a Prusik knot (q.v.); also a hitch or knot whose function depends on friction, e.g. the Tarbuk knot (q.v.).

Front-pointing. A technique used to climb straight up steep snow or ice, by kicking the front points of twelve-point crampons into the slope. An ice-axe in one hand and a peg hammer, or sometimes another ice-axe, in the other hand are used to maintain balance. Front-pointing is a fast but very tiring method of climbing and is usually done in short bursts, with occasional steps to rest. The angles of slopes on

which front-pointing is possible
depends very much on the confidence and strength of the climber
and the quality of the snow or ice.
On hard ice it is rarely posible to
front-point on slopes of more than
50°, but on good snow-ice it may
be possible to front-point on slopes
of up to 80°. Diagram p. 113.

Frostbite. Gangrene that results
from freezing of the tissues. When
the body is exposed to prolonged
cold, ice crystals form in between
the cells, which consequently
become dehydrated, de-ranged and
might even die. The parts of the
body specially liable to frostbite are
the fingers, toes, nose and ears.
Adequate measure should be taken
to prevent frostbite, especially on
the toes which are liable to
become affected if they are cramped
or numbed to begin with by tight
boots and crampons strapped too
tightly to boots.

Recent research into the treatment
of frostbite has shown that the best
treatment is to thaw the frozen parts
slowly, by body heat (such as
putting fingers under the armpits or
in the mouth) or by insertion in
warm water. Hospital treatment of
frostbite includes total immersion in
warm baths and the use of pres-
surized oxygen tents.

The chances of getting frostbite in
Britain and the Alps during the
summer are small, if ordinary
precautions are taken, but it may be
said to be one of the foremost
dangers in high altitude
climbing.

Frost Knot. A knot designed by
Tom Frost, a well known American
climber, for tying the ends of a loop

of nylon tape together, prior to
making the loop into a tape étrier
(q.v.). When finished, the knot
forms a small loop which can be
used to attach a karabiner to the
étrier. Diagram p. 115.

Führerbuch. (*German.*) A record
book; an official note-book carried
by Swiss guides, in which an
employer may record impressions
of a guide's ability and behaviour.
The book is surrendered annually to
the issuing authority for inspection.

Full-weight Rope. Nylon hawser-
laid rope, also called No. 3, with a
circumference of $1\frac{1}{4}''$, a breaking
load of 3500 lbs. and a weight of
$4\frac{1}{2}$ lbs. per 100 foot length. Full-
weight rope is recommended for use
doubled for serious rock climbing,
or singly for mixed or Alpine
climbing not involving extended
rock pitches.

Gabbro. A hard, durable rock of the
granite family, rough and very
sound to handle. The Coolin hills
in the Isle of Skye are the only
considerable extrusions of Gabbro
in the country.

Gangway. A ledge sloping up
across a mountainside or rock face.
Gangways occur frequently on rock
climbs and are usually easy, unless
the ledge slopes outward or if the
gangway is narrow and the retaining
wall overhangs.

Gardening. A colloquial term for
cleaning a rock climb, by removing
grass, vegetation, small trees and
loose rock. This is usually done on
the first ascent of the climb, but in
some cases gardening may go on for

a long time when a climb is particularly dirty. The removal of vegetation often reveals good holds and belays where none appear to exist and usually, the more a route is gardened, the easier it becomes. Many excellent rock climbs, and even whole cliffs, have been developed by the wholesale removal of vegetation.

Gastonade. (*French.*) An amusing and colloquial term used by some French climbers to describe a rock climbing manoeuvre where the climber uses a foothold which is at the level of, or higher than, the hands. Needless to say, this manoeuvre is very gymnastic and has a very limited use.

Gendarme. (*French.*) A prominent pinnacle or tower of rock found mostly on ridges. A gendarme can vary in height from a few feet to several hundred feet. They are usually avoided by a traverse on one flank.

Genevese Abseil. A strenuous and unsafe method of abseiling in which the abseil ropes are passed under one leg and over one crooked forearm only; it is sometimes called the Salève. (See *Abseil.*)

Ghyll, Gill. (*Norse.*) A mountain stream or ravine; also a name occasionally given to a gully climb, particularly in the Lake District.

Girdle Traverse. A route which traverses a cliff from side to side, or as far across a cliff as possible. The girdle traverse of a cliff is not usually done until all the obvious, or natural, vertical lines have been explored. Some cliffs lend them-

selves easily to a girdle, with a convenient series of linking ledges, but on steep cliffs the girdle traverse is often one of the most difficult routes on the cliff, since it crosses walls between existing routes which may be steeper and smoother than most of the cliff. The line of a girdle traverse may wander up and down over large areas of cliff before it reaches the other side, often involving abseils, but by tradition it should not touch the top or the bottom of the cliff before finishing. Difficult girdle traverses demand that the last man of the party should be equally as competent as the leader. (See *Back Rope.*)

Gîte. (*French.*) An old-fashioned bivouac. Before the days of mountain huts parties frequently spent the night above or below the snowline in the lee of some boulders or, at the best, in a rude cabin. The sites of some *gîtes* are well known and are hallowed places in the annals of mountaineering in the Alps. The word is still used to refer to a bivouac.

Glacier. A river of ice, a few hundred yards to many miles in length, which moves slowly down a valley from above the snowline towards the sea under the force of gravity. A glacier is fed by snow falling on the high mountains at its head, which forms névé (q.v.). The névé is constantly subjected to pressure from the weight of further snow and is compressed into glacial ice of a blueish-green colour, which is then carried into the moving glacier stream below. As the glacier descends, the temperature gets higher and the glacier decreases in

*A typical glacier scene, showing a snow peak, a
col, a buttress (centre) and other glacier features.*

size, until the amount of ice melting equals the supply from above, and there the glacier ends. In fact, over the last hundred years or so, most Alpine glaciers have been retreating, which either means there has been a general increase in average temperatures, or that the annual snowfall has decreased. (See *Glacier Snout*.)

Usually the shape of a glacier is tongue-shaped, being broadest at its source and narrowest at its snout. Its general shape conforms to that of the valley in which it lies and its surface reflects uneven sections of the valley floor in the form of crevasses and ice-falls (q.v.). The centre of the glacier is usually higher than its sides, and the cross-section of its surface is thus slightly convex. The surface of the glacier may be covered in moraine (q.v.), formed by stonefalls from the surrounding hillsides.

The moving glacier scrapes along the sides of the mountain on either side and along the valley floor, carving out a typically U-shaped valley. Stones and rubble are embedded in the ice and slowly carried down the glacier. When a glacier melts, particularly at the snout, it releases a tremendous amount of stone and stone dust, forming moraines and giving glacier streams their typical milky colour. Diagram p. 57.

Glacier Cream. A special pigment cream or jelly for smearing on the exposed parts of the body, to give protection from harmful ultra-violet rays and glare from the snow. Serious burns can result from neglecting to use glacier cream in glaciated mountains. The lips, nose and neck are particularly vulnerable.

Glacier Snout. The end of a glacier, where it melts into a lake or a stream. The snout of a glacier is usually very steep, particularly when it falls into a lake and large blocks of ice can break off to form small icebergs. The snout of a hanging glacier may be overhanging and very unstable; falling ice endangers the tracks of parties below these places. Diagram p. 57.

Glacier Table. A block of rock standing on a pedestal of ice on the surface of a glacier; the rock protects the ice beneath it from melting so quickly as the surrounding ice, and thus becomes perched on a pedestal. Diagram p. 59.

Glacis. A plane of rock inclined between horizontal and approximately thirty degrees. A slab is steeper, and a wall is steeper than that. Because of its easy angle, glacis is usually covered in stones and debris and should be climbed with care.

Glissade. A voluntary, controlled descent of a snow slope by sliding and skating on the feet in a standing or squatting position. It is a favourite pastime in mountaineering for it saves a great deal of time on long snow descents and is very exhilarating. The climber should be able to see all the slope below, and make sure that it levels out at the bottom without crevasses and rock outcrops before commencing to glissade. If the snow is too soft and deep or if the slope is not steep enough, a slide may not be possible. If the slope is icy a glissade can easily get out of control and become a fall with possibly serious results. Conse-

Glacier Tables on the surface of a dry glacier.

quently the only really safe slopes for glissading are those which the climber has climbed the same day.

A glissade is made in a ski-running position, with the feet close together and one slightly ahead. The slide may be made either with the feet flush to the slope or on the heels, depending on the condition of the snow and the angle of the slope. The ice-axe is held like a cricket bat, the point at the end of the shaft being pressed into the slope behind the feet to control the rate of descent. Diagram p. 113.

Gneiss. A very stratified rock of igneous and metamorphic origin whose quality is variable. It is perhaps the most inconsistent of rocks from the mountaineers point of view; the mineral composition of gneiss is such that it shatters easily in hard Alpine climates, shedding masses of debris.

Gorge. A deep, narrow valley with very steep sides. Such a feature can constitute a major problem on approach marches in the Himalayas and elsewhere.

Grading of Climbs. Nearly all types of climbs are classified in grades or standards according to difficulty. Each area and each type of climbing usually has a different grading system on account of the varying character of the cliffs and mountains. The degree of sophistication of the various grading systems differs widely, mainly due to the state of exploration of the area but also because of historical associations and even national temperment.

In the simplest method of grading,

the climbs are allocated numbers which ascend with the standard of difficulty; the numerical system is the basis of all grading systems used today and in some areas it is the only system used.

The grading of rock climbs was first suggested in Britain by O. G. Jones in his book *Rock Climbs in the English Lake District,* published in 1897. He suggested in the Introduction to this work the following degrees of difficulty: Easy, Moderate, Difficult and Exceptionally Severe. These four classifications became the basis for the grading of all British climbs, except for certain outcrops which use a numerical system. The classifications used in modern times are as follows: Easy, Moderate, Difficult, Very Difficult, Severe, Very Severe, Hard Very Severe and Extremely Severe. It is virtually impossible to define categorically the difficulties which might be presented by a climb of a particular grade—the system works on a basis of comparison and experience. The grades are allocated by the author of a guide book and despite effort to the contrary, the meaning of the classifications vary from area to area. Sometimes the prefixes of Just, Hard and Easy are used to qualify the grade, but this idea has been generally discarded as being more confusing. Feelings about the grading system vary in Britain—for instance, in Wales, Hard Very Severe, Extremely Severe and even Exceptionally Severe have been in use for some years, whilst in the Lake District, until recently, only Very Severe was used for all the hardest climbs; now, Exceptionally Severe has been dropped in Wales and Extremely

Severe has been adopted in the Lake District.

On certain outcrops, notably the Avon Gorge, Cheddar, Helsby and the South-East England sandstone, a numerical system is used to define the technical difficulty of a pitch. These grades are 1 to 6, with sub-divisions of a, b and c to give an even greater refinement. A recent grading system, developed by R. G. Wilson and P. Crew, combines the adjectival and numerical systems for use on long hard climbs. The numbers are used to define the technical difficulties only and the adjectives to describe the overall difficulties, taking into account seriousness, protection, quality of rock etc. Although this system works very well and is gaining some popularity, it is unlikely to be used widely due to the difficulties of applying the system.

In the Alps there are two main grading systems. In the Eastern Alps, where the climbing is pre-dominantly on rock, a straight-forward numerical system is used. For the more serious and mixed routes of the Western Alps however, there is a more comprehensive system, first developed by Willo Welzenbach in 1925 and later expanded by members of the *Groupe de Haute Montagne*. Rock climbing pitches in this system are graded by a numerical system, illustrated as follows with a rough comparison to British standards:

I — Easy
II — Moderate
III — Difficult
IV — Very Difficult/Severe
V — Severe/Very Severe
VI — Very Severe upwards

The overall grade of the route covers in general the snow and ice difficulties (which are usually very variable), length, seriousness and potential objective dangers. The grades are generally referred to by their capital letters as follows:

F — Facile (Easy)
PD — Peu Difficile (Slightly Difficult)
AD — Assez Difficile (Rather Difficult)
D — Difficile (Difficult)
TD — Très Difficile (Very Difficult)
ED — Extrêmement Difficile (Extremely Difficult)

Of course, the translations have no bearing whatsoever on the English rock climbing adjectival grades. Both the numerical and adjectival parts of this system are sometimes further refined by the addition of *inférieur* (inf.) and *supérieur* (sup.), meaning low or high in the grade. Thus one could have a route graded TD sup., with pitches of V, V sup. and VI inf.

Artificial climbs are graded by the same system in both Britain and on the Continent. The grades used are A1, A2, A3 and sometimes A4 and A5. The opinions of climbers differ widely as to the interpretation of these grades, mainly because of the different methods of artificial climbing used nowadays. The introduction of American equipment and ideas into Europe has revolu-tionised artificial climbing over the last 10 years.

The American system of grading is unique. It is basically numerical, ranging from 1 through 6, with the lower numbers covering walking and various styles of scrambling (with, without rope etc.). The grading of actual rock climbs begins at 5, which is subdivided into 5.1 (*five-point-one*), 5.2, 5.3 etc. up to 5.9 and 5.10, with the higher sub-divisions representing the highest difficulty. Artificial climbing is graded 6 and is subdivided in the same way.

A system for grading snow and ice climbs has recently been developed by the Scottish Moun-taineering Club, for use in their guide books. Because of the very variable nature of snow and ice climbs, such a system can be only very approximate, but it does work to a certain extent. The grades are I to V with the following meanings:

I   — ordinary snow gullies and easy snow climbs

II   — gullies with reasonable ice pitches and easy buttress climbs

III — a wide range covering hard climbing of all kinds; gullies with several ice pitches, buttresses with hard rock and ice pitches

IV — short, but very hard ice climbs

V   — long ice climbs, with sustained difficulties of the highest standard

If full benefit is to be derived from the use of such grading systems as those shown above, various points should be borne in mind. Perhaps the most obvious and important one being that the grading of any climb is given for normal conditions and assuming that the climber has the correct equipment and necessary experience. This point applies particularly in the Alps, where the standard of a major climb can vary from hard to impossible. Also, there are likely to be discrepancies in the grading between guide books, areas

and even between climbs in the same area. The people responsible for writing the guides are experienced climbers and may have done the majority of climbs in his area, but even the most experienced guide book writer relies to some extent on information given to him by other people. Particularly where a climb has not been done often and where the climb is liable to change through removal of loose rock and vegetation, the graded should be treated with reserve.

Granite. An igneous, coarse-grained rock found in many moun-tain and lowland districts. The rock is hard and durable, and its surface is rough—it is admirable for climbing purposes. Granite for climbing in Britain is limited to the Cornish coastlines and some islands and inland areas of Scotland. The best known granite climbs in Europe are the Chamonix Aiguilles in the Mont Blanc range.

Greasy Rock. Lichenous, mossy and grassy rock which becomes very slippery after rain. Climbing in these conditions can be difficult, especially with Vibram-soled boots, and extra care must be taken. Greasy rock occurs frequently in Britain, but rarely in the Alps.

Griff-fiffi. A larger and heavier version of the fiffi hook, with a handle, which makes it much easier to use and hold onto. The griff-fiffi is very useful on artificial climbs where the pitons are already in place, as it effectively gives the climber a few extra inches reach, making it less strenuous to reach pitons. (See *Fiffi, Étrier.*) Diagram p. 50.

Gripped, Gripping. A colloquial term used to indicate that a climber is unusually worried or even frightened, or that a climb is unusually difficult and frightening because of poor rock and poor protection. The term is often used in a humorous sense.

Gritstone. A coarse-grained sandstone, well cemented, firm and durable and found predominantly in the North Midlands and the Pennines. Weathering has revealed gritstone outcrops, mostly as edges and escarpments round the tops of high moors. (See *Edge*.) In the past fifty years thousands of rock climbs have been made on these edges, which are between 15 and 100 feet in height, some of them of an extremely high standard. Gritstone weathers characteristically into rounded bulges and cracks, giving excellent practice in jamming and overhang climbing. The rock is very rough, making it ideal for friction climbing and the use of special rubber climbing boots.

Groove. A place on a cliff where two walls meet at an angle. When this angle is greater than right-angles, the groove is sometimes called a shallow groove; when the angle is more or less at right-angles, the groove may be called a corner (q.v.); when the angle is much less than right-angles, the groove is said to be a vee-groove. In practice the terms groove and corner are applied loosely and are more or less interchangeable. A groove generally has narrower side walls than a corner. The inclination of a groove can be anything up to vertical and even overhanging.

G.H.M. *Groupe de Haute Montagne*— an association of mountaineers founded in 1919 by some of the best French climbers of the day, and derived from the French Alpine Club. The standards of entry are very high and are worked out on a points system—so many points being allocated to all the major Alpine climbs. The Groupe may be joined by people of other nationalities and is now undoubtedly the most competent body of mountaineers in the world, though it may not be completely representative of the best climbers of each nationality. Publishes *La Montagne,* in conjunction with the French Alpine Club, and its own *Annales,* an annual bulletin of information about new climbs in the Alps.

Guide. A professional mountaineer who guides people up mountains. The tariffs are laid down by local organisations in each district or country. Climbing guides in Britain are responsible to the British Mountaineering Council, though though there are a number of independent guides.

Guide Book. A pocket-sized book giving careful descriptions of every rock climb on a cliff, or every route in a group of mountains. The length, grade and details of each climb are given, as well as other general information concerning history, access etc. Guide books are available for all mountain districts in Britain and the Alps and for many other mountain areas in the world. The responsibilities for guide book production are usually taken on by a national or local climbing body, and sometimes by private individuals.

63

Gully. A deep cleft in the face of a cliff or a mountain. Gullies are the most obvious and usually the easiest way up a cliff face and consequently were the first cliff feature climbed in Britain. Chockstones and chimneys are typical features of gullies, which form a natural drainage channel and are therefore often wet and unpleasant. In wintertime, gullies hold snow and ice longer than faces, and so often give excellent climbs, particularly in Scotland.

Gymnastics. A colloquial name for tricky, strenuous rock climbing requiring unconventional techniques. In many ways all hard rock climbs revert to gymnastics at some point.

Hachures. Lines drawn on a map at approximately right angles to the contour lines to represent the shape of the ground. At the top of hills and mountains the lines are close, and they broaden out as the slopes descend. Level terrain such as valleys and plateaux remains white or the base-tint shade of the map. Hachures are no longer used to represent the shape of the land in countries where careful surveys have been made, partly because they cannot be used to represent height accurately and because they interfere with other details on the map. They are still used, however, to represent details of cliffs, quarries etc., which are shown on contoured maps by hachures drawn in a slightly different manner from the original type, and attempting to represent detail by drawing and shading. On large-scale maps of British and Alpine mountain districts, these lines are drawn in

different shades of black and brown with great accuracy to throw into relief the various facets, gullies and ridges which make up the frontage of a steep rock face or mountain. Similarly, blue hachures of this kind show details of ice-falls and crevasses in glaciers. On some French, Swiss and Austrian maps, of a scale 1 :20,000, the detail incorporated using these hachures is remarkable.

Hair-line Crack. A very thin crack in a rock face, which may be merely a scratch and not a crack at all. (See *Rurp*.)

Half-weight Rope. An alternative name for three-quarter-weight rope (q.v.).

Hammock. A hammock specially made for climbers, made from interwoven nylon string or from lightweight nylon cloth reinforced by tape. Hammocks are used for bivouacs on long hard artificial climbs on faces where it is unlikely that a bivouac place will be found. They are used mainly in the Dolomites and in North America.

Hand-jam. The wedging of a hand in a crack to make a handhold. There are two basic ways of doing this, depending on the width of the crack. In fairly narrow cracks the hand can be placed sideways, with the knuckles on one side of the crack and the finger tips pressed against the other. In wider cracks the clenched fist can be inserted, either sideways or vertically. The first is a pressure hold which can be very good, but is usually tiring; the second can be a definite wedge hold

1. (above) *An aerial view of Snowdon, showing a series of cwms, divided by arêtes and ridges. The dark shadows in the back of the cwms are steep, north-facing cliffs.*

2. (bottom) *Cwm Silyn, with its north facing crags forming the back of a typical Welsh cwm, showing ridges, gullies, overhangs, grooves and slabs. The crag is approx. 350 ft. high.*

3. *A typical Welsh rock climb. The author climbing a vertical groove. He is bridging across the groove, using the left hand on a pinch grip and the right hand on a pressure hold. The right hand rope goes through several running belays.*

4. *Stanage Edge, a typical gritstone outcrop.
The climber is laybacking up a flake crack,
protected by a top rope.*

5. Kilnsey Crag overhang, a typical limestone roof, climbed by artificial methods.
The climber is sitting in tape étriers;
the double rope runs through several pitons.
The spare rope is a trail rope.

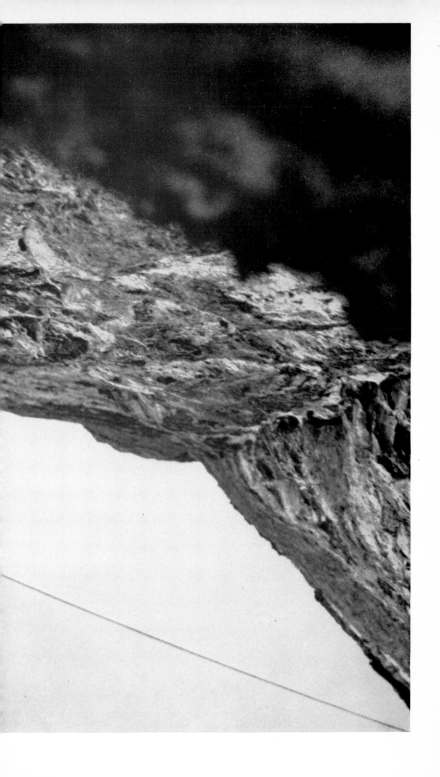

6. *A typical Alpine view. The climber is ascending an ice-bulge on the Forbes arête of the Aiguille Chardonnet. On the left of the picture is a broken rock ridge, with several gendarmes and brèches. In the background is a series of ridges, forming part of the Mont Blanc range.*

7. The Brenva Face of Mont Blanc, one of the largest ice faces in the Alps. The face consists of a series of ridges, separated by couloirs, which have avalanche tracks.

The upper part of the face is a series of hanging glaciers. The lower part of the face is well defined by the bergschrund, which is double on the left-hand side.

8. *A typical summit arête of snow and rocks in the Alps. The approaching party is keeping clear of a small cornice on the right.*

Note the horizontal stratification of the rocks, which are calcareous, and not too sound for climbing.

9. *Ice climbing. The leader is cutting steps with a north-wall hammer. The second is belayed in the shelter of a rock-island.*

10. *Front-pointing up a steep ice slope.*
The climber is using two ice-axes for balance.

11. (above) *A typical snow-bridge in the Alps, across a bergschrund.*

12. (bottom) *A bivouac in the Alps. The climbers are wearing duvet jackets and cagoules and are partly inside a bivouac sack.*

13. *The Chamonix Aiguilles, in the Mont Blanc range, a series of granite peaks giving some of the best rock climbing in the Alps.*

The summit ridges, a complex series of gendarmes, pinnacles and brèches, are almost unique in the Alps.

14. *A typical collection of equipment for two people for a hard Alpine ice climb.*

15. *Abseiling down a vertical wall.*

and if placed correctly can hold the body weight for some time, since its use for upward progress depends more on the arm muscles than the hand muscles. The technique of hand-jamming is one of the most useful and versatile in climbing, since it can be used on a wide variety of cracks with a minimum of effort. (See *Finger-jam*.) Diagram p. 72.

Hand Traverse. A horizontal movement across a rock face, where the body is supported mainly by the hands. Most hand traverses are provided by flakes of rock forming a horizontal crack or by the edge of narrow ledges. Footholds do not exist on a perfect hand traverse and the feet are either hanging free or are used on friction holds to take some weight off the hands. When the flake or holds for a hand traverse rise diagonally, the manoeuvre is always hard and strenuous unless some footholds are available. Some of the hardest hand traverses are to be found on gritstone and sandstone where the handholds are merely rounded ledges which provide only friction holds for the hands. Diagram p. 66.

Hanging Glacier. A minor glacier situated at a higher level than the main valley. The name is applied both to independant units of ice clinging to steep slopes near a summit and to a subsidiary glacier which enters the main one at a steep angle. The latter is usually formed by the differential rate of erosion of the two valleys. The former are often called suspended glaciers—the best examples appear as ice cataracts ending on the edge of a precipice from which large pieces of ice break

away in continuous avalanches. Hanging glaciers can be climbed only with great caution.

Hanging Valley. The valley of a tributary which enters a main valley at a considerable height above the bed of the latter. In consequence, the stream from the hanging valley enters the main valley by waterfalls or rapids. The formation of hanging valleys can either be glacial or post-glacial, by the over-deepening of the main valley.

Harness. The name is generally applied to any form of body harness made from a piece of rope or tape. This may be a temporary harness for the seat and waist, used for abseiling and rescue work, or a specially made harness for the waist or chest, used for tying the end of the climbing rope to the body. The latter type usually have various attachments, such as shoulder straps for extra comfort and various loops and rings for carrying artificial climbing equipment. Some harnesses are specially designed to ensure that the shock load of a fall does not damage the body; some are designed to give maximum aid and support for artificial climbing. Perhaps the most comfortable and best all round harness is the chest type, with shoulder straps.

Harrison's Move. A technique for getting established onto a narrow ledge on a steep wall. This technique commences as a mantelshelf (q.v.) and ends by using one hand on a side-pull to assist standing on the ledge. It is used frequently on sandstone outcrops and derives its name from Harrison's Rocks.

A Hand Traverse.

Hawser-laid Rope. Rope made from three groups of filaments plaited together. The groups of filaments themselves are made up from numerous other groups twisted together. The main advantage of hawser-laid ropes is that the the construction increases the natural elasticity of the filaments. When a load is applied, the filaments tend to straighten out. Hawser-laid ropes made to B.S. 3104 have an extensibility of up to 45%, with an almost complete return to the normal size after a load has been applied. The main disadvantage of hawser-laid rope is that it tends to kink badly, but this can be minimised by careful handling. (See *Rope, Kernmantel Rope, Extra Full-weight, Full-weight, Line* and *Three-quarter-weight*.) Diagram p. 100.

Helm Wind. A strong, north-easterly wind which blows over Cross Fell (2930 ft.), the summit of the Pennine chain, near the border of Cumberland and Westmorland. A long, rolling cloud called the Helm gathers along the plateau-escarpment of the Pennines in this vicinity over which a wind of considerable velocity blows down the scarp face. This moist, violent wind heads towards the Vale of Eden to the south-west, then rises again forming another cloud called the Helm bar, parallel to the Helm and at the same altitude, but a few miles to the south-west over the Vale of Eden. The Helm bar marks the limit of the wind and the disturbance.

Hero Loop. A short loop of nylon rope or tape used as a footloop, in artificial climbing, when the top

rung of the étrier does not give enough height for the next move. Moves using hero loops are usually difficult and strenuous. The name is sometimes used incorrectly for a tie-off loop (q.v.).

Hiebeler Clamp. An alloy device for prusiking, named after the famous German mountaineer Toni Hiebeler. (See *Prusik, Jumar*.) Diagram p. 96.

High Altitude Climbing. The climbing of mountain of more than 18,000 feet high, as is done in South America, Alaska, and Central Asia. High altitude climbing involves considerable hardship, yet it exercises a peculiar fascination over those able to indulge in it, and it is expense and not the fear of hardship that deters more mountaineers from making expeditions to the high altitude ranges. The problems of high altitude climbing are many, including the transport of materials and provisions to remote areas, the lengthy periods of acclimatisation necessary, and the tedious business of establishing and stocking a series of camps on the mountain. Although the highest mountains in the world have all been climbed, some several times (see *Eight-thousander*), there are literally hundreds of high mountains in the world awaiting exploration and ascents. (See *Expedition, Camp, Base Camp* and *Acclimatisation*.)

Hill. An eminence in Britain not more than 2,000 feet high. The definition is arbitrary. A small hill is called a hillock.

Hill-walking. The climbing of

British hills and mountains by walking routes which do not require the use of hands and mountaineering equipment. In fact, nearly all mountains in the British Isles can be walked up, except a few on the Isle of Skye and on the mainland of Scotland. Hill-walking is the first step to mountaineering. It is a school for map reading, compass work, elementary route finding, pace, rhythm and good mountain sense. There are many more hill-walkers in Britain than rock climbers and there are several organisations and clubs for hill-walkers.

Himalayan Club. An international association formed in 1927, "to encourage and assist Himalayan travel and exploration and to extend knowledge of the Himalaya and adjoining mountain ranges through science, art, literature and sport". Its work in assisting expeditions from all quarters in matters of travel arrangements, hire of porters, the provision of interpreters, etc. is widely recognised as invaluable. Publishes an annual journal.

Hitch. A locking and finishing tie knot for additional security.

Hob Nails. Simple, round nails with flat heads fitted to the centre of soles and heels of boots. (See *Nails*).

Holds. Footholds and handholds which enable a climber to ascend rocks. Holds come in many different types and sizes and can be used in many different ways. The main types of holds are treated individually

as follows: Incut, Undercut, Side-pull, Pinch Grip, Jug-handle, Finger-jam, Foot-jam, Hand-jam and Layback.

Holster. A leather or stiff nylon holster designed to be worn on the waistline for convenient carrying and use of a piton hammer or ice axe. Holsters are very efficient and are slowly being used by more and more climbers.

Horizontal Piton. A piton which has its eye at right angles to the blade, so that it can be used in horizontal cracks. The concept and the name are out of date. Nearly all pitons made nowadays are of this type. (See *Vertical Piton*.)

Horn (*German*). A very common name for all sizes and shapes of mountains, especially in Switzerland.

Hut. An erection or building offering sleeping accommodation and an eating place for mountaineers. There are several types of hut ranging from quasi-hotels below the snowline to sparse bivouac huts on the summit of a mountain. The highest hut in the Alps is the Cabana Margherita which stands on top of the Signalkuppe (14,947 feet) of Monte Rosa, closely followed by the Refuge Vallot (14,311 feet) on Mont Blanc.

The huts are usually open to all-comers, but the tariffs are lower and priority of accommodation is given to members of the owner-club and of affiliated clubs. For instance, members of the French, Swiss, Italian or Austrian clubs are entitled to these benefits in the

Alpine huts of all these clubs. British climbers may obtain the same benefits by joining one of the continental clubs, but negotiations are in hand to change this situation. Hut guardians look after the establishments in summer and sometimes food and restaurant facilities are available. These details are published in guide books and it is wise to check, as food and fuel may have to be carried up to the hut and the key may have to be obtained, out of season, from some central point in the valley.

Many British clubs own huts and reciprocal rights for member clubs of the British Mountaineering Council are usually available. British huts offer few facilities other than a place to sleep and cook.

Ice-axe. A tool for cutting and scraping steps in hard snow and ice. It consists of a blade (adze) and a pick forged in one piece and mounted on a wooden shaft from 16 to 35 inches long. A ferrule and a short spike are fitted to the end of the shaft and sometimes a hand strap is fitted, so that it slides up and down the shaft. The overall length of the head of the axe is about 12 inches. Certain French models have collapsible shafts and some have special holes in the adze and pick so that a series of axes can be linked to make a temporary ladder. Most modern ice-axes have a small hole drilled in the head, above the end of the shaft, which can be used to attach a karabiner, or a sling for security. A new type of axe (MacInnes Axe) with a metal shaft is very strong and reliable.

Besides being used for step-cutting

the ice-axe serves as a brake for glissading and arresting falls, for steadying the body in climbing up, down and across steep slopes, as a handhold when it is driven deeply into snow, as a walking stick and for probing crevasses. It is also used sometimes as a belay. Diagram p. 70.

Ice-axe belay. An ice-axe driven into snow or ice to serve as a belay. It is important to drive the axe shaft into a snow slope as far as possible. The belay is made by tying the rope in a clove hitch around the shaft, or by a sling and karabiner if the axe has a hole in the head. On very hard snow and ice it may be impossible to drive the shaft into the slope. In this case, the pick is driven in, so that the shaft lies flush with the slope. This type of belay can work satisfactorily proving a good stance is cut in the slope and the correct technique is used.

Ice Dagger. A specially sharpened piton, or a sharpened piece of metal, with a short sling attached for the hand. The ice dagger is used for additional help when climbing steep slopes, though many climbers now prefer to use an extra ice-axe or piton hammer. Diagram p. 70.

Ice-fall. A cataract of ice formed when a glacier flows over steep ground, round a sharp bend, or between constricting mountain walls. Large crevasses and crumbling towers of ice, called séracs, make ice-falls tricky problems to negotiate and it is best to keep away from the foot of them, which is always exposed to avalanches of ice blocks. If it does become necessary to climb up

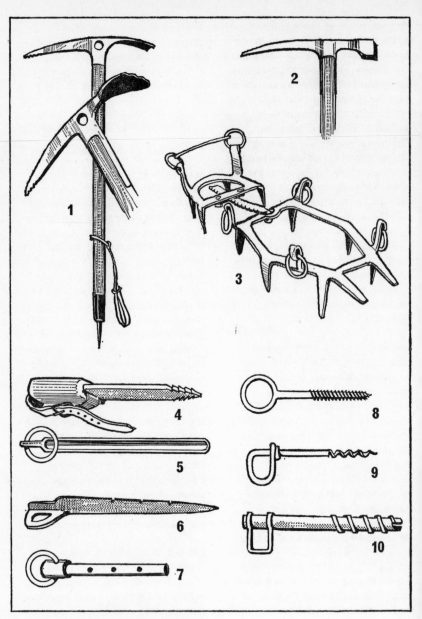

Ice climbing equipment. (1) *Ice-axes, Wrist Sling*
(2) *North-wall hammer* (3) *10-point crampon*
(4) *Ice dagger* (5) *Channel ice-piton*
(6) *Spike ice-piton* (7) *Tubular ice-piton*
(8) *and* (9) *Ice-screws* (10) *Tubular ice-screw.*

through an ice-fall, climbers should always proceed with great caution, roped up and wearing crampons. When expedition routes lie through an ice-fall, this is usually made easier by the use of crevasse bridging equipment (q.v.) and the use of marker flags. Diagram p. 107.

Ice-field. A name loosely used by mountaineers to describe either a large area of ice attached to a mountain face, or to a series of glaciers covering a large summit plateau of one or more mountains. Ice-fields on mountain faces are usually well known since they often constitute a major feature of a climb.

Ice-piton. A piton specially designed for use in hard snow and ice. There are many varieties of which the simplest is a long blade with serrated edges. The most effective type of ice-piton is the tubular kind, but these are very difficult to remove. No ice-piton is as effective as the ice-screw (q.v.). Diagram p. 70.

Ice-screw. An ice-piton with some form of screw formation on the blade. Ice-screws are very effective as they can be used on most types of ice, including water-ice, with a reasonable degree of security and they are very easy to remove after use. Perhaps the best type of screw is the Salewa tubular screw, which is a hollow tube, with a deep screw formation on the outside. Diagram p. 70.

Igneous Rocks. Rocks which have solidified from a molten magma, and form one of the three main types of rocks which compromise the earth's

crust. They may have solidified after reaching the surface, or in channels connecting the molten reservoirs with the exterior, or well below the surface under pressure. In many igneous rocks the various minerals have crystallised separately, and the rock is a mass of interlocking crystals. They do not usually occur in distinct beds or strata, and they are not fossiliferous. (See *Metamorphic Rocks* and *Sedimentary Rocks*.)

Inactive Rope. The rope between any two climbers who are not moving. (See *Active Rope* and *Slack*.)

Incut. A small handhold or foothold, which dips inward to the rock and so provides a good gripping edge for the fingers and toes.

Inserted Chockstone. A piece of rock inserted by a climber into a crack to provide a running belay or a belay. Usually all the necessary chockstones are in place, but on very difficult or new climbs, climbers often carry a small selection of stones, usually rounded or tapered, to insert into cracks. The use of inserted chockstones needs a certain amount of skill in the choice of stones and the choice of position in a crack. (See *Nuts*.)

Instep Crampons. A short pair of crampons with two or four points fitted to the insteps of boots. These are favoured by some climbers for walking up snow slopes, but are rarely used nowadays. (See **Crampons**.)

Ironmongery. A colloquial name for a collection of pitons and other artificial aids (q.v.).

Crack Climbing. (1) *Hand and foot jamming*
(2) *Laybacking.*

Italian Hemp. A type of rope once popular for climbing, but almost completely replaced by nylon. Hemp is still used occasionally for fixed ropes and for top-roping on practice crags.

Jammed-knot. A method of engineering a belay or running belay by tying a knot in a sling and jamming the knot in a crack, in the same manner as a chockstone. A jammed-knot is only used as a last resort, but if the crack has a sufficiently well-pronounced constriction and the knot is tied correctly, it can be perfectly satisfactory.

Jamming. A coloquial name for the use of hand and foot-jams as holds in climbing. (See *Hand-jam* and *Foot-jam*.). Diagram p. 72.

Jug, Jug-handle. Colloquial names for a large hold, usually incut, which can be used by the whole hand.

Jumar Clamp. A mechanical device, made in Switzerland, for prusiking. The Jumar has a pivoting arm which locks against the rope when weight is applied and which releases when the Jumar is slid upwards. It has a handle, to which slings can be attached. Jumars are the most effective device for prusiking, but they have the disadvantage of not working well on iced ropes. Diagram p. 96.

Karabiner. (*German*). An oval or D-shaped link made from steel or light alloy with a spring-hinged gate in one side; it is one of the most useful items of mountaineering equipment. The spring gate of some models can be locked with a revolving threaded screw. Some models have teeth on the end of the gate which engage with a latch on the main body; others rely on the strength of the main part of the karabiner. There are many shapes and designs of karabiners, with varying breaking loads. The breaking load should be stamped on the karabiner; if not, it should not be used for climbing purposes. Most modern karabiners are strong enough for any purpose, though it is advisable to use a karabiner with a screw for belaying and abseiling, for additional security. Some alloy karabiners are designed specifically for artificial climbing, with no teeth, so that they can be opened when under tension.

The main uses of karabiners are as follows: joining the climbing rope to the climbers waistline or harness; joining a belay rope to the climber; joining the loops of an abseil harness; linking the rope to abseil points and running belays, to ensure smooth running; joining étriers and rope to pitons in artificial climbing. In free climbing it is usual for the climber to carry an equal number of slings and karabiners, plus one or two spare for belaying. In artificial climbing up to 50 karabiners may be carried and so it is essential to have alloy karabiners. Diagram p. 76.

Kammkarte. (*German.*) A map in which mountain ridges are shown in plan by black lines. Contours, hachures or any other means of representing high ground, other than spot heights, are absent. A Kammkarte is often produced as a guide to remote mountain areas

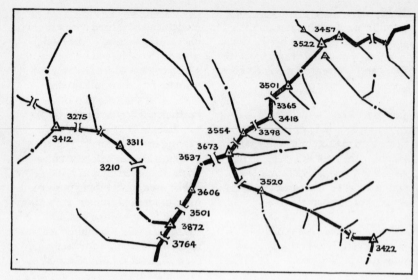

A kammkarte with spot heights.

until a detailed map with contours, etc., is drawn up and it is also used to give a clear idea of the structure of a range in a guide book. Diagram p. 74.

Kernmantel Rope. (*German.*) Rope of a core and sheath construction. The sheath is braided tightly round the core, protecting it from abrasion and other external influences. The core is the actual load-bearing part of the rope and consists of thousands of continuous filaments, lightly twisted together. The main advantage of this type of rope is that it is very easy to handle and does not kink as readily as hawser-laid rope. It has less extensibility that hawser-laid rope (approximately 30%), but this is an advantage for artificial climbing and for use as fixed rope. One difficulty with kermantel ropes is that when abseiling and prusiking, the core tends to move over the sheath, sometimes bunching towards the end of the rope. Certain knots tend to come undone in kernmantel rope and the only really secure knot seems to be the Fisherman's.

The principal sizes of kernmantel rope made for climbing are 11 mm., with a breaking load of 4300 lbs. and a weight of $5\frac{1}{2}$ lbs. per 100 feet, and 9 mm., with a breaking load of 3200 lbs. and a weight of $4\frac{3}{4}$ lbs. per 100 feet. These ropes are intended to be used singly and double, respectively. Smaller sizes are made for use as slings, etc. (See *Rope, Perlon* and *Dodero Test*.) Diagram p. 100.

Khola. A torrent in a deep Himalayan valley.

Kletterschuhe. (*German*). Originally a light, felt-soled boot used for climbing difficult rocks in the Eastern Alps, but now a name for a wide variety of lightweight rock-climbing boots. Diagram p. 28.

Knee Belay. An American method of belaying, where the belayed climber squats, with one leg doubled under, the other arched and the rope is taken in over the arched leg at a sharp angle. A strong grip is needed to hold the rope in the event of a slips and this method is not recommended.

Knife-edge. A very sharp crest on a mountain ridge or the sharp crest of a vertical arête pitch.

Knife-blade. A long thin piton. The name is mainly applied to chrome-molly pitons of this type.

Knoll. A small rounded hill or mound.

Knots. See Bachmann Knot, Bowline Knot, Bowline on the Bight, Double Fisherman's Knot, Figure-of-8 Knot, Fisherman's Knot, Frost Knot, Overhand Knot, Prusik Knot, Tarbuk Knot and Tie Knot. Diagram p. 78.

Knott. An outcrop of rock, especially in the Lake District. It may be a small cliff or a rocky mountain.

Lakes. A shortened name for the English Lake District.

Landing. The last move over the top of a pitch on to a stance, and usually indicated in a guide book if it is difficult. Landing is also used to

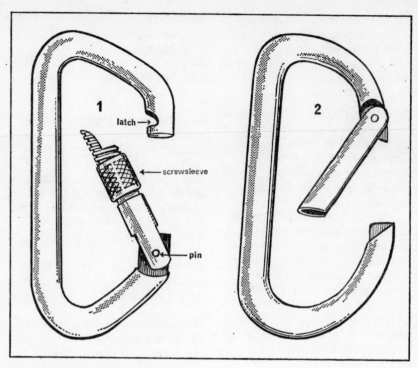

Karabiners. (1) *A typical steel screw-gate karabiner* (2) *a typical alloy karabiner, with no gate.*

describe the area of ground below a climb where the climber might be expected to land if he falls off and hits the ground.

Lark's Head. The conventional name for a tie-off knot (q.v.).

Lassoing. The practice of throwing a rope over a projection to give the leader assistance or protection on a difficult section of climbing. In the Alps this was often done to reach the summits of many smooth pinnacles, unclimbable by other methods available at the time. In these cases, the rope is thrown over the summit and held from the other side, while the leader climbs hand-over-hand up the rope to the summit. Some of these pitches required expert rope throwers; in some cases rocket guns have been used! In Britain lassoing was sometimes used on the first ascents of early climbs, but the majority of these pitches are now climbed free. Nowadays lassoing is used more often than not as a preliminary to a pendulum across a blank wall. Perhaps the most notable example of a lassoo is in North Wales, on Clogwyn du'r Arddu, where the start of a climb consists of lassoing a spike on the lip of an overhang, 30 feet above the ground, and then prusiking up the rope to reach the rock.

Layback. A method of climbing cracks and flakes by gripping the edge with the hands, leaning back and placing the feet flat on the rock at the side of the crack and slightly below the hands. As the climber pulls on the edge of the crack and presses his feet against the rock, the opposing pressures exerted can be sufficient to support the body. Progress is made by moving one hand or one foot at a time. Each movement must be calculated and precise, maintaining sufficient pressure and balance. The layback is perhaps the most strenuous technique for climbing rocks, yet in spite of this it is often the easiest method of climbing a pitch. The disadvantage of a layback is that it is virtually impossible to fix a running belay from this position, so climbers try to avoid laybacking except for short stretches. It is sometimes possible to climb a crack by layback, using hand-jams instead of merely gripping the edge of the crack. This is called a layback on jams. Diagram p. 72.

Leader. The first climber in a party of roped climbers; the leader of an expedition.

Leading Through. The practice of two climbers leading alternately up pitches of a climb. (See *Alternate Leads*.)

Ledge. A level place on a cliff or mountain, which may be grass, rock or snow. Ledges are usually small, or long and narrow—a large rectangular ledge is usually called a platform, a long wide ledge is called a terrace.

Leeper. An American chrome-molybdenum piton, made with a Z-shaped blade and intended for use in fairly wide cracks. The blade is specially tempered, with more spring than usual, so that when a load is applied, the piton tends to grip the crack harder. Diagram p. 94.

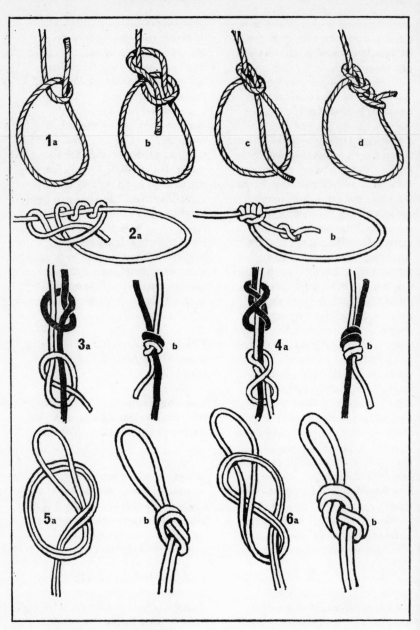

Knots. (1) *Bowline Knot* (2) *Tarbuk Knot*
(3) *Fisherman's Knot* (4) *Double Fisherman's*
Knot (5) *Overhand Knot* (6) *Figure-of-8 Knot.*

Letter-box. A rectangular hole in a narrow rock ridge; a hole formed by jammed blocks or flakes of rock anywhere on a rock face. Letter-boxes of the former type frequently occur on the rock ridges of the Chamonix Aiguilles, in the Mont Blanc range. A small ledge overhung by a jutting rock sometimes offers a constricted stance and may be called a letter-box.

Limestone. An organic rock composed largely of calcium carbonate. The quality of cliffs of limestone varies—some are excellent, others are suitable for climbing only after considerable gardening. Limestone tends to form steep cliffs, often with large overhangs, giving difficult and strenuous free climbing and sometimes very impressive artificial climbs.

Line. The thinnest nylon hawser-laid rope used for climbing purposes, also called quarter-weight or No. 1. Line has a circumference of $\frac{5}{8}''$, a breaking strain of 1000 lbs. and a weight of $1\frac{1}{4}$ lbs. per 100 foot length. It is used mainly for slings and prusik loops, etc., but is gradually being replaced by the use of thin kernmantel rope and tape.

Line Belay. A small belay, a flake close to the rock, or a narrow thread belay which can only accommodate line or some other very thin rope. In general, line belays on spikes and flakes are better made with tape. For fixing thread belays with line, a threader is useful (q.v.).

Livret. (*French*). A record book for French guides. (See *Führerbuch*.)

Long Dong. A special type of Lost Arrow (q.v.) which has a long blade. The blade is almost as deep as it is wide and therefore can be used either way in a crack.

Lost Arrow. An American chrome-molybdenum piton, with a tapering blade and a strong eye forged at right angles to the blade. Lost Arrows vary in size from short thin pitons to long fat ones. Lost Arrows are probably the most useful pitons of any kind. Diagram p. 94.

Longueur de Corde. (*French*). Literally a rope's length; used almost in exactly the same way as the English word pitch. French guide books often use the term to describe a section of easy ground (eg. traverse pour quatre longeurs de corde) which is too easy to require careful description. Unfortunately, when used in this sense it is open to misinterpretation, depending on the climber's idea of a pitch and how far he is prepared to climb on easy ground before taking a stance.

MacInnes Stretcher. A modern mountain rescue stretcher, designed and made by Hamish MacInnes, with many interesting features. The frame is made from Hiduminium alloy tubing, which is both very strong and light; the runners are made from aluminium alloy. The bed is made from terylene netting which doesn't catch the wind and provides a springing effect when sledging a patient over snow or grass. The patient is firmly secured by a comprehensive system of 2″ wide nylon straps and is protected from further damage by an alloy

*A mantelshelf movement,
showing the three main steps.*

headboard and cross members underneath the stretcher. A transport wheel is provided which can be carried separately and easily fitted. The wheel makes transport much more comfortable and faster, even on quite difficult terrain. Perhaps the most important feature of the stretcher is that it folds in the middle and can be carried easily and quickly by one person, even up difficult climbs. The whole stretcher, including the wheel, can be assembled in less than five minutes.

Man. A cairn or rock pillar; a hill with such a man.

Manila. The original type of climbing rope which is lighter than Italian Hemp, but not as strong.

Mantelshelf. A narrow ledge encountered in the climbing of a pitch; the technique to surmount such a ledge. The mantelshelf technique has three main steps as follows: a pull up to raise the body as high as possible; changing one arm, and then the other, into a press-up position; cocking one leg up onto the ledge and slowly standing up. If the ledge is very narrow or sloping, or the wall above is steep and holdless, a mantelshelf can be a very difficult and delicate movement. Diagram p. 80.

Massif. (*French*.) A compact group of mountains, not necessarily a range or a chain.

Medium-weight Rope. An alternative name for three-quarter-weight rope (q.v.).

Mesa. (*Spanish*.) A flat, table-like plateau or mountain, which falls away steeply at all sides. The harder top layers of rock have resisted erosion, and, being practically horizontal, have maintained a surface parallel to the strata. In time a mesa becomes reduced by erosion to a Butte.

Metamorphic Rocks. Rock which were originally Igneous or Sedimentary, but have been changed in character and appearance by the application of heat and pressure, or sometimes by water action. Most common igneous and sedimentary rocks have a metamorphic equivalent. Granite, for instance, may have its principle crystals separated and arranged in crude layers, to become a gneiss; limestone may be re-crystallised to marble; shale may be transformed by great pressure into slate.

Middleman's knot. Any knot with which a climber can tie on to the middle of a rope, including the overhand and figure-of-8 knots, which are the ones mainly used.

Millstone Grit. An alternative name for gritstone, because it was often used to make millstones. Piles of discarded millstones can be seen at the foot of some gritstone edges in Derbyshire.

Mittens. Gloves with a thumb but no fingers which cover the hand entirely; fingerless mittens cover only the wrists and the hands as far as the knuckles, and are useful for rock climbing in cold weather.

Mixed Route. A mountaineering

route in the Alps which involves both rock climbing and snow and ice climbing.

Monolith. An obelisk of rock forming a crack or chimney with the main rock face.

Monsoon. A type of wind system in which there is a complete reversal of the prevailing direction from season to season. The monsoons of India particularly affect climbing in the Himalayas. The intense heating of the land in summer causes a low-pressure area to be established over N.W. India, and the inblowing winds of the south-west monsoon are warm and saturated with moisture. They advance northwards over the region from spring to mid-summer, bringing heavy rainfall to large areas and heavy snowfall in the mountains, particularly in the eastern Himalayas. The south-west monsoon moves forward with a definite front, and arrives at each place at approximately the same date each year. The summer monsoon lasts from about April to September, though its duration at any particular place depends on the geographical location and other factors. Thus climbing seasons in the Himalaya are divided into pre-monsoon and post-monsoon periods.

Moraine. Piles of debris—stones, earth, and rubble—brought down by the movement of a glacier. When rocks fall onto the glacier from the valley sides they form lateral moraines, one on each side of the glacier. When two glaciers meet, two lateral moraines unite to form a medial moraine, which may extend for some way down the centre of

the common glacier. Fragments of rock and debris which are carried in the ice, both as a result of lateral moraine and debris being eroded from the sides and bed of the valley by the glacier, are deposited at the end of the glacier, where the ice melts, and forms a terminal moraine, which may extend across the mouth of the valley. The material of a moraine may vary in size from dust to huge boulders; the rocks are angular in shape and often scratched, since they are dragged and not rolled along by the ice. Old moraines are seen in many districts which were previously glaciated— in many cases the moraines may dam small lakes, particularly in a cirque, or in the lower reaches of the valley where there is a large terminal moraine.

For the climber, moraines can be both useful and a nuisance. Lateral moraines often form easy ways of access up the lower part of a glacier, which may be heavily crevassed, but moraines which are very unstable can be very difficult and tiring to cross or travel on. In popular mountain districts, where the moraines do not change much from year to year, there are often well marked paths along the crest of moraines. Diagram p. 57.

Mountain. A mass of land considerably higher than its surroundings, and of greater altitude than a hill. In Britain, an eminence of more than 2000 feet high is usually considered a mountain, though the definition is arbitrary.

The summit area of a mountain is small in proportion to the area of its base, as distinct from a plateau. Although the highest mountains are higher than any plateau, many mountains are lower than the highest plateaux—e.g. the Tibetan Plateaux, 15,000 to 16,000 above sea level. Few of the highest mountains are single isolated peaks; most of them are arranged in ranges and chains.

Mountains are formed in several ways; by earth movements, by erosion and by volcanic action; though most are formed by a combination of two or all of the factors.

Mountaineering Route. A name given to a few British climbs which, on account of their length, position and variety of climbing, are outstanding or give the impression of an Alpine rock climb. They tend to be ridges or relatively easy classic routes, but the name is used variously depending on the views of the authors of the guide books.

Mountain Rescue Posts and Teams. All mountain districts in Britain and the Alps, and in many other parts of the world, have their own mountain rescue posts. These are located at hotels, huts, police stations, etc., and as such are not manned by full-time personnel. Mountain rescue teams are local organisations made up of climbers who live and work in the district, or who visit it frequently. Their services are voluntary and unpaid. Medical supplies, bandages, splints, stretchers and mountaineering equipment are always available at the posts for immediate use. Some of the teams have their own vehicles, sometimes jeeps and land-rovers and other special equipment such as winches and wire cables, two-way radio sets, etc., which are kept in readiness for use on rescues. If further assistance on a rescue is required, this is often obtained from private parties of climbers visiting the district, from the local police and sometimes from local workers, who may not be climbers. In the Alps, rescue workers, both guides and volunteers, expect payment for helping in a rescue, but this can usually be covered by a special insurance through a climbing organisation. In recent years the helicopter has played a large part in rescues both in the Alps and Britain. In the Alps, helicopters are usually available at most mountain centres as they are used to provision huts, but their services have to be paid for at a very high rate. In Britain, helicopters are sometimes provided by the R.A.F. Mountain Rescue teams, which are located near the major centres. The R.A.F. teams are primarily intended for searching out missing aircraft and personnel, but their services are always made available for civilian rescues.

Details of mountain rescue posts and teams are usually indicated in guide books and in prominent places in mountain areas.

Mountain Sickness. A malady comparable with sea and air sickness which affects people not accustomed to high altitudes, and caused by insufficient acclimatisation, mild forms of sunstroke, exposure to the glare of sun and snow, etc. One of the first signs is the increase in the speed of respiration; headaches, a feeling of nausea, sickness in the stomach and limpness of the limbs are common symptoms. The remedy is for the sufferer to descend as soon as possible, when the sickness will soon pass.

Mount Everest Foundation. After the ascent of Everest in 1953 this foundation was formed by the Alpine Club and the Royal Geographical Society to control the considerable amount of money which accrued through the sales of the book, film and other projects. This money is used to help finance many of the mountaineering and exploratory expeditions which leave from Britain every year.

Move. An upward, downward or sideways movement in climbing. The completion of one move is when both feet and hands have left the original positions and occupy fresh positions. A move is rarely distinguished in a guide book, unless it is particularly difficult or interesting. A phrase such as 'move to the left' may indicate a series of moves.

Moving Together. Using the technique of simultaneous movement (q.v.).

Muggers. A name for clinker nails and hob nails (q.v.).

Mummery's Blood. A concoction of equal parts of rum and Bovril served boiling hot. The recipe was invented by A. F. Mummery, the celebrated late-Victorian mountaineer.

Munro. A mountain in Scotland more than 3000 feet high, defined as 'separate' by Sir Hugh T. Munro in the now celebrated Munro's Tables of 3000 feet Mountains of Scotland.

It must not be confused with a top, which is a summit more than 3000 feet high, but not classed as a separate mountain by Munro. A Munro may have several tops. According to the tables there are 276 separate mountains of over 3000 feet in Scotland, and 543 tops. A small number of climbers and walkers have ascended all the Munroes—the barriers to this achievement are not so much the technical difficulties as the remoteness of the mountains and the consequent time involved in reaching them.

Muscle-up. A colloquial term for making a strenuous move using mainly arm and finger strength. Climbing in this way may be unavoidable, but often it is the climber's technique that is at fault, by climbing too fast, or not using the feet properly on small footholds.

Nails. Nails designed for mountaineering and fitted to boots. It is also used colloquially for nailed boots. Nails have now almost been completely replaced by the use of Vibram and other composition soles, but are still used occasionally by older mountaineers and by some Scottish climbers, who prefer nails to crampons for winter climbing in Scotland. Diagram p. 85.

Natural Line. A rock climb which follows an obvious feature up the face of a cliff, such as a groove, a gully or a series of cracks. A natural line has no bearing on difficulty, but tends to give more continuous climbing which reduces artificiality to a minimum. A route may also be said to follow a natural line if it

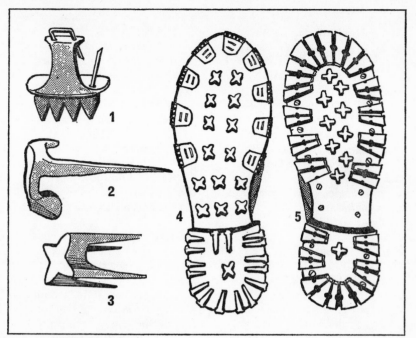

Nails and Vibram soles. (1) Tricouni Nail
(2) Clinker Nail (3) Mugger Nail (4) a typical
nailing pattern with Tricouni edge nails and
Muggers on the sole and Clinker edge nails on
the heel (5) Vibram sole and heel.

takes the easiest line up a complex
face. Such a route may be devious
and of a varied character, but it is
usually inescapable and considerably easier than other climbs on the
same face.

Needle. An upstanding pinnacle
of sharp rock, with a sharp top.
One of the best examples in Britain
is the Napes Needle on Great
Gable in Cumberland, which was
the scene of one of the earliest rock
climbs in Britain, by W. P.
Haskett Smith in 1884.

Natural Thread. A place for a
thread belay made by a natural
formation of the rock, as distinct
from a chockstone, such as a
temporary closing of a crack or a
hole through a piece of rock. The
latter type of natural thread occurs
frequently on limestone, through
water erosion.

Neb. A jutting overhang or roof of
rock, particularly on gritstone.

Nevado. (*Spanish*.) A peak in the
Andes, particularly in Peru. Two
other common names are Cerro and
Nudo.

Névé. (*French*.) Permanent snow
lying at the head of a glacier; snow
which lies in cirques and on the
slopes of high mountains and never
melts. The névé at the head of a
glacier feeds the main ice stream,
may conceal crevasses and is
usually cut by a bergshrund.
  The snow in névé gradually
changes character, due to the
pressure of a great depth of the
snow, which depresses the freezing
point. The snow in the lower layers

thus melts, and solidifies again into
granular ice. As the glacier moves
down the valley the névé gradually
becomes welded into a completely
crystalline mass of ice. Diagram
p. 57.

Niche. A small recess in a rock face,
which is usually large enough to
hold a climber. Niches are noted
particularly by guide books when
they form a difficult section of a
climb, or when they provide a
stance or even a bivouac place.

Nobble. A method of putting a
climber off his stride by making
disparaging remarks about his
ability, his style, or the difficulties
and dangers of a climb. Nobbling is
usually only done by groups of
friends climbing in a competitive
spirit on outcrops, or problem
climbs. It is sometimes used by
local climbers to upset a well-known
visiting climber, who may be trying
to ascend some notorious local
climb or problem. Nobbling, of
course, is nearly always carried out
in a friendly and joking manner!

North-wall Hammer. The name
given to a special ice-axe, which has
a hammer head instead of the adze.
The principle of the north-wall
hammer is that the pick is used for
cutting steps in ice and the head for
driving ice-pitons. The use of
north-wall hammers is fairly limited
as most climbers prefer to carry both
an ice-axe and a piton hammer. On
some types of climbs however, the
north-wall hammer is the ideal tool
for ice climbing. Diagram p. 70.

Nose. A jutting nose of rock,
broad and sometimes with an under-

cut base. It may vary in size from a few feet to many hundreds of feet.

Number One, Two, Three and **Four.** Names for the various sizes of hawser-laid nylon ropes, as defined by B.S. 3104. (See *Rope*).

Nunatak. An isolated mountain peak or hill projecting from an ice-cap, as in Greenland and the Antarctic. The nunataks become more numerous towards the edges of an ice-cap, as the ice there is thinnest.

Nuts. In recent years the technique of using inserted chockstones has been greatly extended by the introduction of a series of artificial metal chockstones. The original metal chockstones were simply nuts, with the thread drilled out to prevent chafing on the sling, which could be threaded onto a sling—a great advantage over carrying a pocketful of loose chockstones. Apart from the ease of carrying, the fact that the sling goes *through* a nut, instead of *round* a chockstone, often makes the running belay more mechanically sound. Several nuts of different sizes can be carried, sometimes with two or three nuts on a single sling, thus vastly widening the range of potential running belays, as nuts can be inserted in shallow cracks and pockets where it would be impossible to use a normal chockstone.

Nowadays several types of special aluminium metal chockstones are made of all shapes and sizes, with one or two holes drilled through for the sling. A few are illustrated on page 88. Some people regard these devices as artificial aids, as they can be hammered into cracks much in

the same way as a piton and indeed often dispense with the need for pitons, but their use has become widespread and accepted as a normal free climbing protection device.

Nutting. A technique similar to chockstoning (q.v.) but with the use of nuts.

Ö.A.V. *Oesterreichischer Alpen Verein*—Austrian Alpine Club, founded in 1862, with headquarters in Vienna. (See also D.Ö.A.V.). In London there is a commercial agency operating as representatives of the Ö.A.V., through a travel agency.

Objective Dangers. Dangers in mountaineering which are not the result of faults in the climber's technique. These include falling stones, avalanches, crevasses, ice-falls, etc.

Offset. A type of blade piton made from a flat piece of steel, with the eye made in an offset portion bent at right-angles to the blade. The name is used particularly for the American chrome-molybdenum pitons of this type, which are made in several sizes. Some of these sizes have special names (see *Knife-blade* and *Bugaboo*). Diagram. p. 94.

Ordinary Route. A colloquial name for the usual or the easiest way up a cliff or a mountain, particularly when there are routes nearby with similar names endorsed 'direct' and 'eliminate', etc.

Orography. The branch of physical geography which deals with mountains.

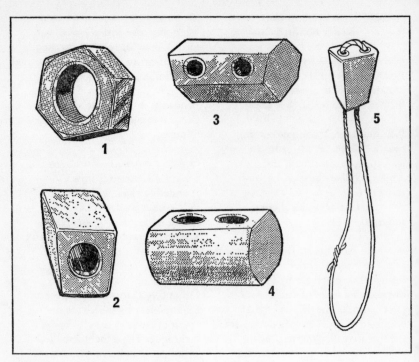

Nuts and alloy chockstones. (1) *Nut* (2) *Troll* Spud (3) *Clogwyn* Clog (4) *Peck* Cracker (5) *Moac* chockstone.

Outcrop. A small cliff. Every mountain has outcrops, but few of these are climbed because of the proximity of larger cliffs. The outcrops climbed extensively in Britain are the sandstone, gritstone and limestone cliffs in south-east England, the Midlands and the Pennines. Outcrop climbs are short and difficult, offering good practice for more ambitious climbing elsewhere. Many sea-cliffs have also been developed in the same way as outcrops, particularly in Cornwall.

Outcrop Climber. A climber who frequents outcrops, or a particular outcrop, either because he prefers to climb on small cliffs rather than mountains or because of the difficulties involved in travelling regularly to a mountain area. The term is often used in a derogatory sense.

Overdrive. A piton is said to be overdriven either when its effectiveness is reduced by too much hammering and consequent damaging of the crack, or when it is hammered past its point of optimum usefulness. This latter point applies to hard artificial climbing, particularly with the use of chrome-molybdenum pitons. A piton can be inserted by an experienced climber, so that it is strong enough to hold the body weight, or even a fall, whichever is required, but it is possible to overdrive a piton, making it very much stronger, but also much more difficult to extract, which can waste a considerable amount of time on a long artificial climb.

Overhand Knot. The knot used by a climber to tie himself onto the middle of a rope. A loop is gathered in the rope and a simple overhand is tied in it. The knotted loop can be dropped over the head and shoulders and adjusted around the waist, or it may be clipped into a karabiner attached to a waistline. The overhand knot is also used for tying the climbing rope to a karabiner on a belay sling. (See *Figure-of-8 Knot*.) Diagram p. 78.

Overhang. Rock and ice beyond the perpendicular. The climbing of rock overhangs is strenuous but not necessarily difficult if good holds are available and the correct techniques are used. In general it is best to keep the feet on the rock and the body bunched up, but on some overhangs it is possible to bridge out and attain a position of equilibrium. Ice overhangs are usually serious problems and can only be climbed by artificial techniques.

A sharp overhang, near or on horizontal, is called a roof (q.v.).

Oxygen Equipment. Light-weight oxygen apparatus sometimes used on high altitude expeditions in the Himalaya, to combat the lack of oxygen in the atmosphere. The equipment, which is carried on a pack-frame, consists of one or more cylinders of oxgen, with valves, breathing tubes and masks. Two main types of apparatus have been used in the Himalaya: the open circuit set from which the climber breathes a mixture of pure oxygen from the set and air from the atmosphere; the closed circuit set with which the climber breathes only pure oxygen from the set, exhaling through a soda-lime canister which separates the carbon dioxide from the exhaled gases and returns surplus oxygen to a breathing bag.

The degree of revival afforded by using oxygen apparatus has to be counterbalanced against the additional weight of the equipment, and the margin of benefit derived only effectively reduces the altitude by a small amount. The present feeling about oxygen for high altitude climbing seems to be that it is essential for medicinal purposes, useful for sleeping and dispensible altogether for climbing.

P.A.'s. Lightweight rock climbing boots with canvas sides and smooth rubber soles, designed by Pierre Allain, a well-known French climber. These boots were originally intended for use on the practice crags of Fontainbleau, but have gained wide acceptance in Britain for all types of hard climbing. P.A.'s fit the foot closely and are excellent for friction and crack climbing.

The original model of the P.A. boots are now made under a different name; there are several, usually inferior, imitations on the market. (See *Socks*.) Diagram p. 28.

Pack-frame. A carrying frame, usually made from light alloy tubing, which is designed for carrying heavy loads in a comfortable manner. The loads may be loaded into a fixed bag on the frame, or strapped onto the frame separately. Unfortunately many pack-frames are badly designed and they are not very popular with mountaineers. Diagram p. 102.

Parka. A type of anorak or wind

jacket with a fur lined hood and possibly a fur lined body.

Pass. A deep depression between two mountains. In Britain a few passes are crossed by good roads and most are crossed by good paths. The name 'col' is also used by climbers for high mountain passes in Britain.

Passage. (*French.*) A pitch (q.v.). It can also be a succession of pitches forming part of a route in the Alps, and constituting a notable feature of the climb.

Paying Out. Paying out the active rope to a moving climber. Just sufficient rope and no more is payed out as a climber moves; too little can result in a jerk on the climber, too much slack may foul on projections or increase the length of a fall. (See *Belay* and *Taking In*.)

Peak. The top of a mountain, especially when it is sharp. Also a shortened name for the Peak District of Derbyshire.

Peel Off. A colloquial term for falling off a climb.

Peg. A colloquial name for a piton. A piton hammer is often called a peg hammer; artificial climbing is often called pegging.

Pendulum. A sideways movement across a rock face by swinging on a rope suspended from above. The rope may be fixed to or thrown over a rock projection or a piton, above or to one side of the line of climbing. The climber then swings on the rope across to a ledge or a fresh line of holds a few feet away. A very long pendulum might involve several swings back and forth, literally running across the rock face, to gain sufficient momentum.

Perlon. A German trade name for nylon. Often erroneously used by climbers to indicate that a rope is of kernmantel construction (q.v.). (See *Rope*.)

Pied d'Elephant. (*French*.) A waist length bag for protecting the lower part of the body on bivouacs. The bag may be made from waterproof nylon, intended for use in conjunction with a cagoule; or it may be a short sleeping bag, for use with a duvet jacket.

Pigott Stretcher. A makeshift stretcher made from a climbing rope and designed by A. S. Pigott. It is useful for carrying climbers with minor injuries, but is not suitable when a patient has spinal injuries, etc.

Pike. A sharp mountain, particularly in the Lake District.

Pillar. A detached rock or cliff with a flat summit.

Pinch Grip. A small vertical hold, with two sides but no top. The hold is used by gripping one side with the fingers and the other side with the thumb and exerting a lateral pressure, which is sufficient to keep the climber in balance whilst making a move. If the sides of the pinch grip are incut, the hold can be very effective; otherwise the hold relies on friction. Pinch grips can sometimes be used on very sharp vertical arêtes.

Pinnacle. A slender rock tower, tapering towards the top. The name is often used in Britain for any detached or distinct piece of rock.

Pitch. A section of climbing between two stances or belay points. Rock climbing pitches may be chimneys, cracks, grooves, slabs, walls, etc., each giving a different style of climbing, though a pitch may well have a combination of several features and styles of climbing.

The length of a pitch is determined by the frequency of ledges and belays, the amount of rope available and the difficulty of climbing. On easy climbs, where there are usually frequent ledges and belays, the length of any pitch is entirely up to the leader—he may stop at every ledge and belay, if he is leading a party of novices, or he may climb several sections in one rope length to save time. Guide books usually break down easy climbs into short pitches, but as the length of each pitch is given, it is easy to calculate if two pitches can be run into one. A further limitation on pitches of easy climbs may be that two or even three climbers may be tied at intervals on the same piece of rope, thus necessitating the use of very short pitches. Harder climbs are usually steeper and with less available stances, so pitches tend to be longer and more clearly defined than on easy climbs, and there is less opportunity to vary the pitches on a climb. It is interesting to note that over the last 10 years or so, the 'standard' length of rope used by climbers has increased from 100 feet to 120 feet, and from 120 feet to 150 feet. Even on the hardest climbs, both in Britain and in the Alps, it is unusual to climb for more than 150 feet without coming across a good stance. There are notable exceptions, of course, of free climbs with pitches of 200 feet or more—these are usually climbed on 300 foot lengths of rope, or an artificial stance is made at some convenient point on the climb, to enable it to be climbed with 150 foot ropes.

On artificial climbs where ledges are the exception rather than the rule, the length of a pitch often depends on the quality of the rock and pitons. Belays are usually only made in places where several good pitons can be inserted. (See *Belay Seat*.)

The length of a pitch, as quoted in guide books, is always the length of climbing and not the direct distance between two stances. Thus a pitch between two stances 50 feet apart may be 70 feet in length, consisting of 50 feet of vertical climbing and 20 feet of traversing. The length of a climb is given as the sum total of the length of the individual pitches.

When climbers are moving singly on snow and ice the length of pitches is a matter for the leaders judgement. In gullies, the pitches might be determined by physical features, but on open faces a stance can be made almost anywhere, by cutting a stance in the snow and belaying on an ice-axe or ice-piton.

Piton. A piece of metal designed to be hammered into a crack in a rock face, to serve as a belay, a running belay or an artificial aid. All pitons have either a fixed eye or a loose welded ring, which protrudes from the crack when the piton has been inserted. A karabiner can be used to link the rope or an étrier to the piton.

The shape and size of pitons vary widely, so that all types of crack can be used. The smallest pitons fit hair-line cracks and the largest fit cracks of up to four inches wide (see *Angle, Bong-Bong, Blade Piton, Bugaboo, Channel Piton, Crack-tack, Knife-blade, Leeper, Long Dong, Lost Arrow, Offset, Universal*, etc.). Diagram p. 94.

Pitons are made mainly from two materials—mild steel and chrome-molybdenum steel—with a few others made from stainless steel and aluminium alloys. The design and materials used for pitons are primarily governed by the type of rock for which they are to be used. For example, Cassin pitons made in Lecco are of mild steel, have a limited range of sizes and are intended for use in the Dolomites; Simond and Charlet pitons made in the Chamonix valley are also made of mild steel, have a wider range of sizes and are intended for use on Chamonix granite. However, the best designed and strongest pitons are those made from chrome-molybdenum steel, an idea originally conceived by John Salathe for use on the granite walls of Yosemite in California. These pitons are now made by a number of American and European firms. Chrome-molybdenum pitons are made in a full range of sizes and have the great advantage of being so strong that they can be used over and over again—a great advantage on very long artificial climbs. Because of the undoubted superiority of this type of piton, they are now used by many climbers to the exclusion of all other types. Recent research has shown that only pitons of chrome-molybdenum steel have the necessary holding power to withstand a fall in free climbing (about 4000 lbs.) and that mild steel pitons are only advisable for artificial climbing. Chrome-molybdenum pitons are initially more expensive to buy, but worked out on a usage-cost basis, they are far cheaper than mild steel pitons.

The ideal placement for a piton is in a horizontal or inward sloping crack, with the eye as close to the rock as possible—this takes advantage of the mechanical position of the piton, as well as its inherent holding power—but careful placement in a vertical crack may be adequate. On artificial climbs, the ideal placement of any piton is that which will support bodyweight comfortably—placing a piton too hard in a crack only means that valuable time is wasted in extracting the pitons (see *Overdrive*). A ringing sound from the piton normally indicates that the piton is well placed and in good rock. A dull sound indicates poor placement or bad rock, but even a piton in bad rock may be usable if the placement is mechanically sound. The use of pitons is highly skilled and takes much practice to become fully conversant with all the techniques involved. (See *Artificial Climbing, Coupled Pegs, Expansion Bolt, Tie-off.*)

Piton-carrier. A loop of wire or light metal bar, either like an enlarged key-ring, or with a small spring gate, which can be used for carrying several pitons. The piton-carrier is attached to a sling or the waistline. Diagram p. 94.

Piton Hammer. A hammer

specially designed and carried for inserting and extracting pitons. The sizes weights and shapes of piton hammers vary widely depending on personal preference and the type of climbing for which the hammer is intended. Some hammers have a double head, others have a short flat spike, or a long spike, which can be used for chipping flakes, gardening and even for ice climbing. The weight of piton hammers varies from 12 to 25 oz.

Plan. (*French.*) A level bed in the bottom of a deep Alpine valley, or a large level area on the shoulder of a mountain.

Platform. A large rectangular ledge usually used as a stance.

Pocket. A small round handhold into which one or more fingers can be placed. These are common on sandstone and gritstone as a result of water erosion.

Porphyry. An igneous rock of granitic composition, hard, durable, purple and brown in colour and ideal for rock climbing. Much of it is found with rhyolite in British mountain districts.

Powder Snow. Fresh snow which has neither thawed nor been re-frozen. Its texture is fluffy and it gives a characteristic squeak underfoot. Powder snow is dangerous on steep faces, and can be very tiring to walk through.

Press Up. An upward movement on rock completed by pressing down on the palms of the hands on

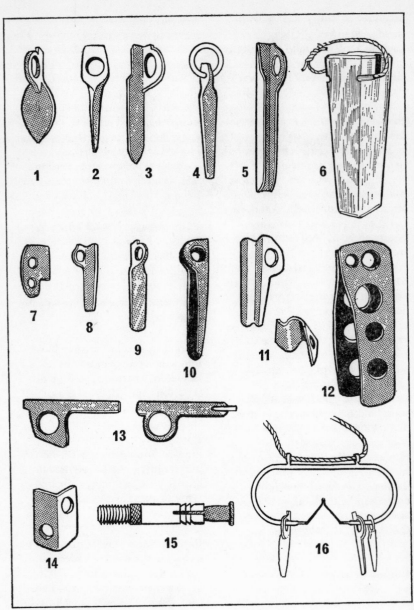

Pitons. (1) *Ace of Hearts* (2) *Universal*
(3) *Blade* (4) *Ring or Abseil piton* (5) *Channel*
(6) *Wedge* (7) *Rurp* (8) *Offset* (9) *Lost Arrow*
(10) *Angle* (11) *Leeper* (12) *Lightening
Bong-bong* (13) *Expansion bolts with eyes*
(14) *Fish plate* (15) *Expansion bolt needing
fish plate and nuts* (16) *Piton Carrier.*

large flat holds and ledges. (See *Mantelshelf*.)

Pressure Hold. Any foothold or handhold used to maintain a position on a rock face by exerting pressure sideways and downward on them. Pressure holds in chimneys and corners may not be holds at all, for the feet and hands are pressed against the smooth walls of rock.

Protection. The quality and number of running belays available to safeguard a pitch. Pitches are said to be poorly protected and well protected according to the circumstances. A climber is said to have good protection technique if he is particularly skilled at fixing running belays.

Prusik. The technique of climbing a rope by means of prusik knots or some similar device. Two prusik knots are used on the rope, one attached to a chest harness or the waistline, the other as a footloop. The climber rests on the upper knot, which is attached to the body and raises the lower knot, which is the footloop. He then stands up in the footloop and moves the upper knot up the rope. Prusiking is slow and strenuous unless the climber is well practised in the technique.

Prusik Knot. A friction hitch which is attached to a climbing rope as a means to climb the rope when escaping from a crevasse or when climbing a fixed rope. When strain is put on the knot it jams on the rope; when the strain is released the knot can be pushed up the rope. The prusik knot is usually made with a long loop of rope which can

be used as a footloop, or attached to the climbers harness or waistline. Several mechanical devices exist for the same purpose (see *Hiebeler Clamp*, *Jumar Clamp*). Diagram p. 96.

Psychological Belay. A poor belay or running belay, which is used when nothing else better is available to give the leader confidence to continue with the climb. Psychological belays are rarely used, as the belay is such a fundamental safeguard, but a leader may use a psychological running belay instead of a piton, if he is climbing well and full of confidence.

Pull Up. A strenuous upward movement on good handholds and usually with few or no footholds to assist the movement.

Quarter-weight Rope. An alternative name for line (q.v.).

Quartz. A mineral rock, white and light-grey in colour. Quartz occurs on many cliffs in Britain, mostly in the form of veins; some pitches can be covered in quartz. Care in handling is required as much of it is brittle.

Quartzite. A metamorphic rock, representing a recrystallised sandstone, which occurs on a few cliffs in Scotland and on Anglesey. The quality of quartzite can vary, but it is usually very hard and very compact, with few good cracks for pitons.

Quebrada. (*Spanish*.) An Alpine valley. The name is used mainly in the northern Andes.

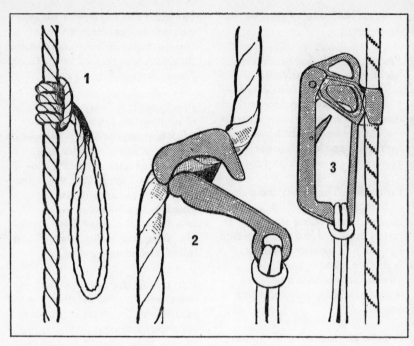

(1) *Prusik Knot* (2) *Hiebeler Clamp* (3) *Jumar Clamp.*

Rake. A rising ledge across a cliff face. Rakes are usually covered with grass and debris and may form shallow gullies. They provide scrambles and a rope is not usually required.

Range. A line of mountain ridges, with or without peaks, in which the crests are relatively narrow; if the altitude is comparatively low, the ridges may constitute a range of hills rather than of mountains.

Râteau de Chèvre. (*French*.) A steep flake of rock rising against a vertical wall, such as is often found in the Chamonix Aiguilles. A râteau de chèvre can be climbed either by an ascending hand traverse, or by inserting one arm and one leg and wriggling upwards.

Ravine. A deep cleft in a mountain-side and the floor of a valley. It tends to be narrower than a gorge and with steeper sides. Some ravines give long gully climbs.

Recess. A niche or a short corner in a rock face. The name is used loosely to indicate any feature of this type.

Règlette. (*French*.) Literally a ruler. A long thin narrow hold, as may be formed by the top of a thin flake, on which the finger tips of both hands can be placed.

Ressaut. (*French*.) A bulge or a steep rise in a rock ridge.

Reversing. Climbing down on rock. It is a general principle in mountaineering that a climber should not make a move on a rock face which he cannot reverse. This applies to all but the hardest climbs. In Britain it is rarely necessary to climb down rocks, unless one has decided to abandon the ascent of a climb and there is no belay or running belay immediately available for a descent aided by the rope. In the Alps, however, some descents involve long stretches of climbing down rocks. The main point about reversing on rock is to select the lowest handholds before stepping down. Reversing is generally easier and less strenuous than climbing, except on hard and steep climbs. On very easy rocks, it is preferable to reverse facing outwards.

Rhyolite. An igneous rock of granitic composition, grey-brown in colour and ideal for rock climbing. It is found in Britain with porphyry in the best climbing districts.

Rhythm. Controlled, balanced movements in walking and climbing. Good rhythm is the secret of effortless mountaineering. A steady pace in walking and slow deliberate movements in climbing are the basic requirements for rhythm.

Rib. A short, steep rock ridge, with short sides and a sharp or blunt crest.

Ridge. The line on which two faces of a mountain meet. It may be rock, snow, or ice, or a combination of these. Ridges are major features of all cliffs and mountains, and offer a wide variety of problems. The crest of a ridge can vary from a broad rounded slope, to a sharp rock edge. Diagram p. 39, photographs 1, 6.

Ring Piton. A piton with a loose

A typical Roche Moutonée.

welded ring instead of a fixed eye. These are intended primarily for abseiling—the ring helps to reduce friction on the rope when it is recovered. Ring pitons are not satisfactory for normal use as the ring can be easily damaged when inserting and extracting the piton. Diagram p. 94.

Roches Moutonées. (*French.*) Rounded outcrops of rocks in glaciated valleys, so called because of their likeness to sheep's backs. These outcrops are the result of glacial erosion. They are worn smooth and sometimes scratched by the movement of the glacier. The side facing up the valley is usually at a gentle angle; the side facing down the valley is shorter and steeper. Roches moutonées are often crossed on approach marches in the Alps and may be troublesome to ascend at times. Diagram p. 98.

Rognon. (*French.*) Literally kidney. A large island of rock in the middle of a glacier. An ice-fall or crevasses may result from a rognon constricting the flow of the glacier, and the island itself may be a safe route through the ice-fall to the upper part of the glacier. Rognons are often used as resting places, bivouac sites and even as hut sites.

Roof. A sharp overhang, near or on horizontal. Small roofs are relatively easy to climb, if there are good holds available on the wall above, which can be reached while the climber is still in contact with the wall beneath the roof. Large roofs constitute major climbing problems. Some roofs, with good jamming cracks

and flakes, can be climbed free, but most require the all out use of artificial climbing techniques. Diagram p. 20, photograph 5.

Rope. Rope made to certain specifications, for use in mountaineering. There are several types and sizes of rope, all with different characteristics and with specific purposes.

The ropes originally used for mountaineering were made from Italian Hemp and Manila. This type of rope has several serious disadvantages—its breaking load is relatively low, the material has little resilience or elasticity and it absorbs 50% of its own weight of water, resulting in a serious loss of pliability. Also the fibres deteriorate rapidly, unless kept under ideal conditions. Since the advent of nylon ropes, hemp ropes have largely fallen into disuse and are now only used perhaps as safety ropes for outcrop climbing and by inexperienced climbers who know no better.

Nylon, as a material, is almost ideal for climbing ropes. It is relatively strong (see breaking loads under the various sizes), it has a high elasticity which means it is capable of absorbing a great deal of energy in a fall, it is resistant to abrasion and it is hardly affected by damp and sunlight. One major disadvantage of nylon is that it melts easily and so a climbing rope should never be allowed to run over another piece of nylon when any load is on it.

There are two main methods of construction of nylon ropes (see *Hawser-laid Rope* and *Kernmantel Rope*). Until recently all British-made ropes were hawser-laid. Kernmantel

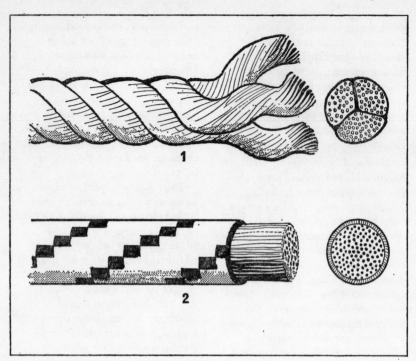

Ropes. (1) *Hawser-laid rope.* (2) *Kernmantel rope.*

ropes were first developed on the continent and are now used by a growing number of British climbers. The specifications for climbing ropes are carefully defined and manufacturers of climbing ropes have to state clearly, on a label attached to the rope, that it has been made to these specifications. Any rope which does not have such a label, should not be used for mountaineering of any kind. In Britain, the specification is B.S. 3104 (1959), which was worked out in conjunction with the British Mountaineering Council. On the continent, ropes have to come up to a standard defined by the U.I.A.A. (see *Dodero Test*). Both these specifications are under constant revision.

Ropes are expensive and a vital piece of equipment for the mountaineer. They should be regularly inspected for damage by cuts and abrasion, internal wear, and damage from chemicals and heat. Any rope which has sustained a fall should be rejected.

The lengths of rope used for climbing vary. In Britain the standard lengths are 120 feet and 150 feet, with continuous lengths of 240 feet and 300 feet sometimes used for artificial climbing and abseiling. On the continent, the standard lengths are 30 metres (100 feet), 40 metres (130 feet), and 50 metres (165 feet); with the continuous double lengths for artificial and abseiling. It is common practice to have half of a double length rope, or one of the two double ropes, dyed a different colour to the other so that it may be easily distinguished in use. (See *Extra Full-weight*, *Full-weight*, *Line*, *Three-quarter-weight* and *Perlon*.) Diagram p. 100.

Rope Management. The technique of managing climbing ropes in any manoeuvre on a cliff and mountain. (See *Back Rope*, *Paying Out*, *Taking In*, *Tension Climbing*, *Tension Traverse*, *Waist Belay* and *Shoulder Belay*.) There should never be any slack rope between two climbers when one is moving, and accumulated slack rope should be piled or coiled neatly if possible on the stance being used. If the stance is small, slack rope can be let down the cliff face provided there is no chance of it catching in a crack, or on a flake or overhang. If there is any doubt, the rope should be coiled onto the knees and jammed against the rock to prevent it falling. When the leader has completed a pitch and his second is due to bring up a third person lower down, the rope between the leader and the second man should be pulled up by the leader to avoid confusion and tangling with the rope between the second and third man.

In artificial climbing rope management can become very complicated, unless the climbers are experts. To assist rope management in artificial climbing, when using doubled ropes, one of the ropes is usually dyed a different colour, so that the leader and second can refer to the ropes without confusion. A leader may require protection or tension on one rope and slack on the other.

Rope management by the leader is relatively straightforward, as long as he ensures that the rope runs freely through running belays and round corners, by the use of slings. When using doubled ropes, care must be taken not to cross the ropes between running belays or pitons.

Rope off or **down.** Colloquial terms

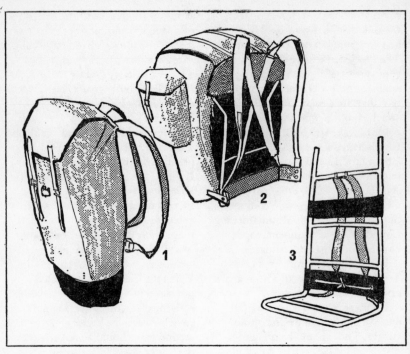

Rucksacks. (1) *Frameless climbing sack*
(2) *Frame sack for walking* (3) *Pack-frame.*

for abandoning a route by means of an abseil (q.v.).

Roping Up. The action of a party of climbers tying themselves together with climbing ropes at the foot of a climb or mountain.

Roture. (*French.*) The gap left by a glacier along its sides, often caused by the warm rocks melting the ice.

Route. A particular way up a cliff and mountain. A route may not necessarily involve roped climbing.

Route-finding. Finding the way up a cliff and mountain—one of the fundamental arts of mountaineering. Route finding in the British Isles is rarely difficult in clear weather providing a walker can use a map and compass properly, though in bad weather and winter in some mountain areas a fair amount of skill is needed. Similarly, there is little difficulty in following most British rock climbs as most are carefully described in guide books and there have been so many ascents of straightforward routes that trails of scratches mark the rocks.

In the Alps and further afield, however, the problems of route-finding, particularly on snow and ice mountains, can be acute. It needs a great deal of experience and a certain knack to find the easiest and quickest route through difficult country and up extensive mountains. Obviously a person with local knowledge will be in a far better position than a complete newcomer to an area. Guide books to Alpine regions assist up to a point, but they leave much for the individual to resolve on his own. Route-finding is

perhaps the biggest problem for a novice in the Alps.

Route of Character. A rock climb or mountaineering route which is outstanding because of its historical associations, or its high quality. Routes of character are often steep, varied, continuous and often difficult and inescapable except for roping off. The phrase is a favourite expression, used by guide book authors, to describe the best climbs. (See *Classic Route.*)

Rubbers. A colloquial name for rubber-soled gym shoes, which were once very popular for climbing difficult routes in Britain. Climbing in rubbers on dry rocks is easier and more pleasant than wearing boots; in fact, in some old editions of guide books, routes were graded for ascents in rubbers. They have several disadvantages, however, on small incut holds and on wet rock. With the advent of P.A.'s and similar footwear, and their widespread use in Britain, the use of rubbers has diminished considerably. (See *P.A.'s* and *Socks.*)

Rucksack. A bag fitted with shoulder straps and designed to be carried on the back. There are many designs of rucksacks, but the two main types are those with frames and those without. Frame rucksacks have some form of metal frame to which the bag and straps are attached. The frame rests on the back, which is protected by webbing straps, and it helps air to circulate between the sack and the carriers back, thus preventing condensation, and it prevents the load from digging into the carriers back. Framed rucksacks are used mainly by walkers; they are unsuitable for climbing because they tend to roll on the back. Frameless rucksacks are made for mountaineers. They fit the back snugly, giving freedom of movement of climbs. Because the load is closer to the back, it exerts less force on the shoulders. The main disadvantage of a frameless sack is that it has to be packed very carefully, to prevent the load from digging into the carrier. This can usually be avoided by putting a sleeping bag or clothing against the back. Frameless sacks for Alpine climbing are fitted with various attachments for carrying ice-axe, crampons, etc., on the outside of the sack (See *Pack Frame*.) Diagram p. 102.

Runner. A colloquial name for a running belay.

Running Belay. A belay through which the active rope runs at an intermediate point between a moving climber and a fixed climber, to reduce the potential falling distance of the former and to give him confidence to make difficult moves. Running belays are used to protect leaders on vertical climbs and to protect both the leader and the second on traversing climbs.

The principle is quite straightforward. In the case of, for example, a 50 foot wall pitch with two good rock spikes at 15 and 40 feet above the stance at its foot, the leader climbs the wall putting slings on both spikes in turn. The climbing rope is then clipped into a karabiner attached to the loops, which allows it to run freely as the climber progresses. If the leader falls off between the first and second spikes, he can

only fall a theoretical maximum distance of 50 feet (allowing, for the sake of argument, that the climbing rope is not allowed to run), instead of a potential 80 feet without a running belay. Even if the sling or belay should break, it will still serve to absorb some of the energy of the fall. If the leader falls off above the second spike, the potential falling distance is reduced to 20 feet. Runners not only give physical protection, but, and probably more important, also confidence to do a difficult move a long way up a pitch. The same principle applies to traverses, where potential swings by both the leader and second can be reduced by the use of runners.

A leader carries a collection of slings of various lengths and sizes, and possibly a collection of nuts and pitons, to take advantage of any protection a climb may offer. On straightforward climbs only a few slings, of heavy rope, may be carried; on a difficult climb up to twenty slings may be carried, with the majority of them thin rope or tape. (See *Sling, Tape, Chockstone, Nuts*.) Diagram p. 120.

Run-out. A colloquial name for a pitch, being the length of rope required to climb it. The phrase is also sometimes used to describe a part of a pitch where there are no running belays available; e.g. 'it is a long run-out to the next runner'.

Rurp. The Realised Ultimate Reality Piton—a very small American chrome-molybdenum piton, designed for use in hair-line cracks. The rurp has a very sharp edge and is specially toughened so that it can be literally smashed into a crack. The rurp does not have a conventional karabiner eye (the piton is too small)—instead it has a small hole drilled into it, through which a short loop of thin nylon or kernmantel can be threaded. Rurps are used only on the very hardest artificial climbs and despite their tiny size, they can be very effective for direct aid. Diagram p. 94.

Sabots. (*French.*) Wooden clogs or felt shoes provided for visitors at large Alpine huts, to help keep them clean and to prevent damage to wooden floors.

S.A.C. *Schweizer Alpen Club.* (See *C.A.S.*)

Saddle. A shallow depression in a ridge or a broad shallow col.

Safety Rope. An independant rope attached to the climbers waistline when he is making an abseil. This is paid out by another climber at the abseil point.

Sandstone. A sedimentary rock consisting mainly of fine grains of quartz cemented together. The colour of the rock may be yellow, brown or red. Some sandstones are poorly cemented and therefore readily disintegrate on exposure to weather. The main sandstone outcrops in Britain are in the south-east, notably Harrison's Rocks and High Rocks, and in Cheshire, notably Helsby and Frodsham Edge. The style of climbing on these outcrops is predominantly one of strenuous finger climbing on walls and overhangs, with a notable absence of cracks suitable for jamming. The climbing is very

specialised and it calls for gymnastic and unorthodox moves. Because of the friable nature of the rock and the extreme difficulty of most of the climbs, it is usual for them to be climbed on top-ropes, even by local expert climbers. This practice is prevalent on the outcrops in south-east England, where there are usually trees along the top of the crags, forming convenient belays. The technique used is for a belay to be fixed on the tree and the rope passed through it and held from the ground, so that the belayer may join in the fun of watching the antics of the leader. At Helsby, the rock is of better quality and there are no trees, so top-roping is only used by inexperienced climbers, or on the hardest climbs. Rubbers or P.A.'s are used on sandstone, as boots would quickly destroy the holds.

Scarpetti. (*Italian.*) Light, rope soled boots, similar to Espadrilles (q.v.).

Scoop. A shallow oval scoop, or a rounded niche, frequently found on gritstone and sandstone outcrops. The bottom of a scoop is usually flat, or a very easy slab angle, and steepens towards the top.

Scramble. Climbing on easy broken rocks, usually without a rope.

Scrappy. A colloquial description of rock climbs which are uninteresting, usually on account of grassy sections between pitches making the climb discontinuous.

Scree. Zones of boulders and small stones covering a steep slope below a steep face. Slopes of scree are invariably tedious to ascend. The size of the stones varies; large stones generally form stable scree, which is reasonable for uphill walking, small stones generally form loose scree which moves underfoot and can be very tiring. In Britain scree tends to lie in bands of one size of stone—smaller stones accumulate in gullies and shallow scoops as they gradually fall down the mountainside.

Scree-running. A rapid descent of a steep slope of scree by running and sliding through the stones. The stones must be small and fairly loose to make scree running worthwhile. Scree-running is exhilarating, but wears boots out very quickly.

Season. Used colloquially by climbers to indicate the summer mountaineering season in the Alps. If a climber makes a number of important or worthwhile ascents in a summer, he is said to have had a good season. (See *Winter Ascents*.)

Second. The second person on the rope in a roped party of climbers. To second a climb is to do a climb as the second man on the rope.

Sedimentary Rocks. Rocks which have been deposited as beds, often as sediments (i.e. under water), forming one of the three types of rock which make up the earth's crust. They are laid down in distinct layers or strata, separated by bedding planes, mainly by the sea, but also by lakes, streams and even by the wind. Among the common forms of sedimentary rocks are Gritstone, Limestone, Sandstone and Shale.

Sentry-box. A name sometimes

given to an angular recess on a rock climb, in which the climber can stand. They often provide stances.

Sérac. (*French*.) A pinnacle or tower of ice in an ice-fall. Séracs are continually forming and falling with the movement of the glacier and because of melting during warm weather. Great caution is necessary to negotiate a barrier of séracs and they are best crossed at night, or when the glacier is well frozen. Diagram p. 107.

Seven-thousander. A colloquial name for a mountain of greater altitude than 7,000 metres (22,966 feet). There are hundreds of seven-thousanders, all situated in the Himalayas and central Asia, of which well over a hundred have been climbed. Aconcagua, the highest mountain in South America, was long thought to be the only mountain on the American continent to exceed 7000 metres, but recent surveys have shown that the height of the mountain is somewhere in the region of 6960 metres.

Shelf. A small platform or perhaps a large mantelshelf.

Sherpa. A native of the Sola Khumbu district of Eastern Nepal. Originally of Tibetan stock, these sturdy men have proved themselves invaluable to high altitude expeditions in the Himalayas. They are notable for their endurance, particularly at high altitudes and many sherpas have taken part in the ascents of some of the highest mountains.

Shoulder Belay. A method of

A rope of climbers negotiating a barrier of séracs in an ice-fall.

taking in and paying out a belayed active rope under one arm and over the opposite shoulder. The shoulder belay is particularly useful for bringing up seconds and for holding a leader who has fallen without a running belay. The dynamic belay operation is difficult to apply when using a shoulder belay, but many climbers at home and abroad still prefer to use it. Diagram p. 123.

Shoulder, Giving a. A colloquial expression for giving the leader some assistance to start a pitch, by allowing him to stand on ones back, shoulders or head. (See *Combined Tactics*.)

Side-pull. A vertical handhold which is used by leaning away in the opposite direction. Side-pulls are not very positive holds, but they are frequently used to assist balance in delicate manoeuvres. (See *Pinch-grip*.)

Sierra. (*Spanish*.) A high range of mountains with sharp outlines. The name literally means a saw.

Simultaneous Movement. The action of a party of roped climbers moving together over rocks, snow or ice. The technique is used mainly when climbing on easy angled snow slopes, when there may be some danger of crevasses. The climbers are spaced out evenly at intervals of 10 to 30 feet, and the rope is held taut by the rearward climber who prevents it from trailing on the slope and becoming entangled with the leader or any obstructions. The rope is held in the hand with three or four coils of spare rope held loosely, which can be released or gathered in

to allow for fluctuations in the pace of the party. The ice-axe is held in the other hand, ready to be driven through the coils of rope into the slope in case of a slip or a fall into a crevasse. This method of climbing saves a great deal of time, provides a certain amount of security and may be used on quite difficult ground by experienced climbers.

Basically the same idea is used on easy rock, except that when one of the party comes to a section needing the unencumbered use of the hands, the other members of the party take a temporary belay and take the rope in as normal. Simultaneous movement on rock needs careful attention—to the rope, to the other members and to loose rocks, etc., which may be dislodged.

Simultaneous movement is essential in all branches of Alpine climbing to ensure that climbs are done as quickly as possible. The more experienced a climber is, the more he will be able to move simultaneously, and the quicker and safer he will climb. Some experienced climbers prefer to unrope completely on easy ground and solo, but unless the easy sections are long, this is rarely worthwhile.

Ski-mountaineering. The sport of climbing mountains on skis, especially in winter time.

Sky-hook. A very advanced artificial aid, which consists of a flattened hook of high quality steel. The hook can be used on the edge of tiny flakes, ledges or horizontal cracks, or on the edge of steep flakes, which have been chipped to give a small notch. Sky-hooks have a small eye, to which a sling and étrier can be attached. They are used mainly by climbers in North America, particularly in the Yosemite valley, and frequently avoid the use of expansion bolts. They are particularly useful on loose flakes, which cannot be used for conventional holds and which would probably break off if a piton was used. Diagram p. 118.

Slab. A plane of rock inclined between 30 and 75 degrees to the horizontal. The definition is loosely applied. Slabs are one of the most common types of rock problem and they give delicate climbing in all degrees of difficulty, mainly on flakes, incut holds and flat-topped ledges. Smooth slabs require good friction technique and confidence.

Slack. The rope on a stance ready to be paid out to a moving climber; the rope taken in and accumulated on a stance from a moving climber; the amount of rope allowed to slacken accidentally when paying-out—the result of bad rope management. 'Slack!' is also a call for more rope from a moving climber to permit manoeuvres on a pitch.

Sleeping Bag. A body length bag filled with feathers or down, used for camping and bivouacing. (See *Duvet*.) Diagram p. 46.

Sling. A short length of rope or tape, tied into a loop and carried round the neck with a karabiner, used for belaying, running belays, abseils, etc. The length of slings vary, but they are usually 5 feet, carried singly, or 9 feet, carried double. Heavy slings are carried for belaying and a range of slings of all sizes, possibly with nuts attached, are carried for

running belays. Slings can be linked together, or to pitons, to prevent the rope from binding when it runs over an overhang or round a sharp corner. Slings should be tied with a firm knot (Fisherman's or Tie Knot) and should be regularly inspected for damage and to ensure that the knot is firm. It is commonsense to use the largest and strongest sling possible, particularly when belaying.

S.M.C. Scottish Mountaineering Club, formed in 1889, to encourage mountaineering interests in Scotland. Has rooms in Edinburgh and Glasgow, owns several huts in Scotland and publishes a series of guide books and an annual journal.

Snow-blindness. A temporary blindness caused by snow-glare and ultra-violet rays. It can be a very painful condition and is best avoided by the careful use of good quality snow goggles.

Snowbridge. A bridge of snow spanning a crevasse or bergschrund, formed by a partial collapse of the snow concealing the hole. The quality of snow bridges varies immensely. Sometimes they have to be crossed, as they may be the only means of crossing a crevasse or a bergschrund unless a long detour is made. If there is any doubt about whether it will take the weight of a climber without collapsing, it is advisable to take belays and for the party to cross one by one, on all-fours or even by wriggling across in a prone position.

Snow Cups. A common formation on snow surfaces caused by intense evaporation at high altitudes. The snow becomes indented with millions of little cups rimmed by sharp crests, like miniature craters.

Snow-field. A large expanse of permanent snow, some of which may be névé.

Snow-goggles. Tinted lenses in aluminium frames, or spectacle frames with side hoods, which protect the eyes from snow-glare and ultra-violet rays. The frames or hoods prevent the light from filtering around the side of the lenses, though condensation can become a serious problem unless some ventilation is allowed for. Snow-goggles should be worn at all times for crossing snow and glaciers, and even for climbing rock peaks in glaciated regions; without them eye-strain, sickness and snow-blindness can quickly develop.

Snow-ice. Ice formed from wet snow which has frozen and compacted. Snow-ice is ideal for climbing —it is easy to cut steps in, it is very strong and is perfect for front-pointing.

Snowline. The general level (altitude) at which snow begins to lie permanently on a range of mountains. Due to differences in altitude, varying climates and relative positions to the equator, the level of snowlines of mountain ranges differs considerably, and the level can vary in the same range. Thus on the north and west slopes of the Alps the snowline is about 9500 feet, and on the south and east slopes 10,000 to 10,500 feet above sea-level. By comparison, the snowline of mountains near the equator is 15,000 to

17,000 feet and in Scandinavia 4000 feet.

Socks. An abbreviation for climbing in socks pulled over rubbers or P.A.'s, which is sometimes done on wet or greasy pitches. On slabs, a climber may simply remove his boots and climb in stockinged feet.

Socle. (*French.*) An introductory buttress. The name is usually used for a fairly easy angled buttress which abuts against a steep spur or a steep wall.

Solo Climbing. Climbing alone and unroped. Solo climbing may be practised by experienced mountaineers on climbs which they know to be well within their own limits. It is a very exhilarating experience, but can be dangerous. A climber on good form can ascend difficult rocks solo in very rapid times.

Some climbers make a habit of climbing long difficult routes in the Alps solo. This may involve the use of auto-protection techniques, where the climber uses a loop of rope clipped into pitons, ascending and descending in turn, to clip and unclip his rope to the pitons.

Spindrift. A powder snow avalanche or powder snow being blown by the wind. Spindrift occurs mainly in winter and can make climbing very unpleasant and even dangerous. It is a common condition on Scottish winter gully climbs.

Spot Height. The height of a peak, or some other notable feature, shown on a map as a spot with the height alongside. Large scale maps give spot heights at frequent intervals on mountains, on points along ridges, the edges of glaciers, at the foot of ridges and spurs, etc. These are very useful for determining height differences, or the altitude reached, particularly on long Alpine climbs. (See *Kammkarte*.) Diagram p. 74.

Sprag. A type of finger hold used in very thin cracks, where only the tips of the fingers can be inserted. The thumb is pressed against the edge of the crack, or against the wall if it is a corner crack, in opposition to the force made by the fingers.

Spur. An extended buttress of a hill or mountain, usually small and rounded.

Staircase. A rock pitch rising up a series of steps, often found in the beds of gullies.

Stance. A place on a mountain or a cliff where a climber can stand or sit in reasonable comfort and manage a rope; a stance usually has one or more belays available, but when a piton belay has to be used these are often found already in place, left by previous parties. The size of a stance can vary from two good footholds to a large terrace, and in between we find platforms, ledges, niches, sentry-boxes, and a variety of con-stricted positions in chimneys and behind large flakes, or astride the level crests of ridges, pinnacles and flakes, all of which may be used as stances. Comfort is the climber's main consideration when taking a stance, as he may be there for some time and a belayed climber cannot manage the rope properly if he is precariously balanced or sitting in a painful position.

When no stance is available on a steep climb, an artificial stance can be made by using étriers or a belay seat (q.v.).

Standard of Climbs. Grading of climbs (q.v.).

Step. A sudden rise in a ridge.

Step-cutting. Cutting and scraping of steps for the feet in hard snow and ice with an ice-axe or north wall hammer. This is done when a slope becomes too steep for walking up or down in boots and crampons, or when it is too tiring for step-kicking. Steps are cut slightly incut to prevent the feet slipping off them. The size of a step cut depends on the angle of the slope and the confidence of the party; in descent, or if the steps are to be used subsequently in descent, larger steps than usual are cut. If possible, steps should be cut with the adze of the ice-axe, but if the snow or ice is too hard the pick has to be used, which usually requires many blows. On a moderate slope where balance can be maintained, the climber should stand upright and use both hands when cutting steps; where the slope is very steep, it is better to lean inwards on one hand and cut the steps with the other. For steep difficult climbs, many climbers prefer to use a very short axe, which can be wielded easily by one hand.

Cutting steps downhill is more difficult than cutting uphill because balance is more easily upset by clumsy movements and considerable practice is needed before the correct sequence of foot movements on the steps cut is found.

Even when wearing crampons,

steps may still be cut for additional security, particularly on hard ice. (See *Crampons* and *Ice-axe*.) Diagram p. 113.

Step-kicking. Kicking steps in snow. This method of ascending and descending snow slopes saves time over step cutting, but can be very tiring unless the snow is in ideal condition. The toes are thrust downwards into the slope with each movement, with the axe driven into the slope to assist balance. When descending, steps can be kicked facing outwards with the heels, unless the slope is steep, when the climber will have to face into the slope.

Steps. Steps cut or kicked on snow and ice.

Stomach Traverse. A technique of traversing ledges which are over-hung by steep rocks. This is done by lying prone on the stomach and wriggling along the ledge. The whole body may be on the ledge, or the feet and legs may be hanging free outside, if the ledge will not accommodate the whole body. Such a manoeuvre is unusual on high mountains, but common enough on British outcrop climbs.

Stone-falls. An objective danger in high glaciated mountains, caused by the melting of snow and ice dis-lodging stones and pieces of rock. Couloirs are notorious for falling stones, being natural funnels for collecting the loose material which falls from the surrounding faces. The best time to cross and climb such couloirs is at night, or very early in the morning before the sun reaches

the face and begins to melt the snow and ice. In any event, certain risks are run no matter what time of day couloirs are climbed, so they should be climbed as quickly as possible to minimise any risk.

Stone-shoot. A scree-filled gully, usually without pitches, and which may be suitable for scree-running if the stones are small enough.

Stoptout. (*French*.) Gaiters used by climbers. There are several types— short stoptout, which cover the ankles and the top of the boots are very useful for stopping small stones and scree from getting inside the boots. Long stoptout cover the calf of the leg and the top of the boots and are used to keep the legs and feet warm and dry in deep snow, and when climbing high mountains. Stoptout are usually elasticated and some have zipped sides, so that they can be put on and taken off without removing the boots.

Straddling. A bridging movement across a gap, in a chimney, groove, etc., or a long stride between holds on a face climb.

Strenuous. A description given in rock climbing to a move, a pitch, or a climb which requires forceful climbing by pulling with the fingers and arms. Holds far apart, or poor holds, on walls, in smooth chimneys and cracks, on overhangs, etc., are responsible for strenuous climbing. It means strenuous despite the use of good technique. An inex-perienced, or off-form climber, may find many climbs strenuous.

Style. A climber's style in climbing

Ice-climbing techniques.
(1) *Step cutting* (2) *Front-pointing*
(3) *Glissading* (4) *Braking a fall.*

rocks and ice. There are good and bad styles, which reflect good and bad technique. Bad style usually results in a climber finding a climb more strenuous and difficult than he would by using good style. Easy graceful movements enhance style. (See *Dynamic Posture* and *Technique*.)

Swami-belt. A waistline made from several turns of wide tape and used mainly by American climbers.

Taking In. Taking in the active rope from a moving climber. The rope is taken in so that it is just tight at the climber's waist; slack rope will get in the way of the climber and may foul on projections. When the climber moving gets into difficulties he may ask for the rope to be taken in tight, to give him some support and to stop a fall immediately, should he fall off. (See *Belay* and *Paying Out*).

Tape. Nylon tape or webbing, of various widths used for mountaineering. The sizes of tape used vary from $\frac{1}{4}''$ wide to $2''$ wide. Most of the tape is flat, but some, particularly that used by North American climbers, is tubular. Tape has several advantages over normal slings, in certain uses. On rounded spikes and knobs tape has less tendancy to roll off. When using a thin flake for a running belay, a tape of the equivalent size to a rope sling will be much stronger. When used as abseil or direct aid slings, tape is much more comfortable to use. Tape is also used for a variety of other purposes, such as tie-off loops, hero loops, étriers and harnesses.

Soft tape is better than hard tape, mainly because knots in hard tape tend to come undone very easily. There are special knots for use with tape. (See *Tie Knot* and *Frost Knot*.) Diagram p. 115.

Tarbuk Knot. A friction knot, designed by Ken Tarbuk, for use with nylon rope. It is used to attach the end of a climbing rope to the climber's waistline by means of a karabiner. The main advantage of this knot is that the active side of the knot, on which the load comes, is straight. Most knots bend the rope into a sharp angle, which reduces the strength of the rope by quite a high percentage—this is avoided in the Tarbuk knot. When there is no load on the knot, it can be slid up and down the rope easily, making it very easy to adjust belays to the correct tension. When a load is applied to the knot the turns of the knot bind more tightly on the rope—an advantage with nylon which is very slippery. When a very heavy load is applied to the knot, such as when a leader falls, the knot will slide on the rope, thus enhancing the effect of the rope stretching and dynamic belay techniques in absorbing the energy of the fall. Diagram p. 78.

Tarn. A small mountain lake. The word is used particularly in the Lake District.

T-bar. A device for belaying in snow, designed and made by Hamish MacInnes. It consists of two pieces of T section alloy, about $16''$ long, bent at an angle of about $45°$ to each other. One section is for hammering into the snow; the other section lies flush with the surface and has an eye for attaching the belay.

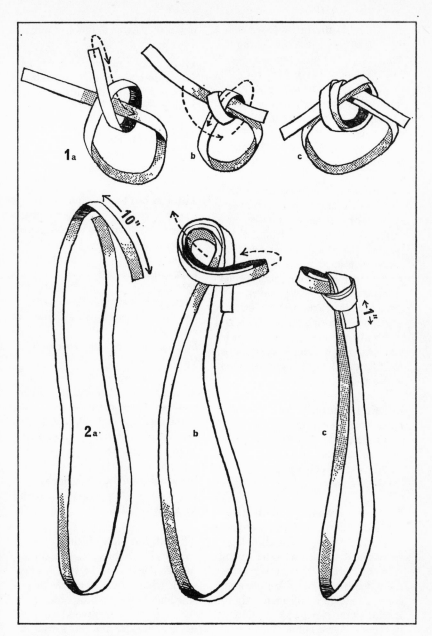

Tape Knots. (1) *Tie Knot for slings*
(2) *Frost Knot for étriers.*

Technical Difficulties. Essentially the difficulties in mountaineering which demand the ability to apply good technique in climbing rocks, snow and ice. Technical difficulties are distinguished from psychological and logistical difficulties which might be encountered on long climbs. Short rock and ice climbs are often called technical problems.

Technique. The correct methods and their variations of overcoming all types of rock, snow and ice problems. These range from balance, posture, selection of holds, and their correct use, application of the various methods of climbing special features such as crack, grooves, laybacks, etc., to the arts of rope management, using artificial aids and protection methods, cutting steps in snow and ice, walking on crampons, etc. Good technique is synonymous with style.

Tension Climbing. An alternative name for artificial climbing, using two ropes, and using tension from the rope to assist the leader in resting and moving up. (See *Artificial Climbing*.)

Tension Traverse. An alternative method to the pendulum for crossing a steep smooth wall. The climbing rope is held in tension by the second man and the leader progresses across the traverse by using side-pulls and friction holds, leaning against the tension of the rope, which is slowly paid out by the second. Many free climbs involve tension traverses, and in this context they are not regarded as artificial climbing.

Terrace. A large ledge running

across the face of a cliff or mountain.

Thin. A colloquial term signifying that a climb is very delicate, or that a section of a climb is climbed on very small holds.

Thirty-fives. The 370 summits of the Alps which exceed a height of 3500 metres (11,483 feet).

Thomas Stretcher. A mountain rescue stretcher, standard equipment at most mountain rescue posts, made from duralumin tubing with wooden runners. It is made to be kept and carried assembled. A special splint, designed to be used with the stretcher is available. The handles are extending to allow the carriers to see where they are putting their feet. Side straps are provided for additional helpers.

Thread Belay. A hole, formed by a chockstone or a natural constriction in the rock, through which a sling can be threaded to make a belay or a running belay. The sling is passed double through the hole and retrieved from the other side and the two ends are clipped together with a karabiner.

Threader. A piece of stiff wire used to assist in the threading of a sling on awkward thread belays. The end of the wire is usually bent into a small hook, for catching hold of the rope. There are several ways of using a threader. If a chockstone is deep in a crack, the sling can be thrown over the chockstone and the bottom recovered by the threader. If the hole to be threaded is very small, the threader can be bent into a half circle and threaded through first. The rope is then attached to the threader which can be used to pull the sling through the hole. It is not unknown for threaders to become jammed in very small holes and climbers, in desperation, have used them as handholds or even as a running belay.

Three-point Climbing. A basic principle of rock climbing, which is essential on all but the easiest of climbs. It means that only one leg or arm must be moved at a time to make progress, leaving the other three limbs to maintain balance and contact with the rock. There are, however, certain techniques such as hand traverses, pull ups, etc., which use only two-point climbing.

Three-quarter-weight Rope. Nylon hawser-laid rope, also called No. 2, with a circumference of $\frac{7}{8}''$, a breaking load of 2000 lbs. and a weight of $2\frac{1}{2}$ lbs. per 100 foot length. Three-quarter-weight rope is used principally for artificial climbing (always doubled) and sometimes for Alpine mountaineering, not of a serious nature. It is used frequently for slings. Other names occasionally used for three-quarter-weight are medium-weight and half-weight.

Through Route. A passage or hole behind a chockstone or jammed block, often avoiding difficulties on the outside.

Tie Knot. A knot specially designed for use with tape. It is exactly the same as a Fisherman's knot, but with the two halves of the knot intertwined. The tape is kept flat and the resulting knot is neat and tidy. Its name comes from its similarity to the knot used to fasten a tie. Diagram p. 115.

Tie-off. A method of reducing the leverage on a piton which has not been fully inserted, by tying a short loop of rope to the piton blade, close against the rock face. When doing hard artificial climbs a number of small loops are carried for this purpose. Diagram p. 118.

Tiger. A colloquial term for a mountaineer who consistently climbs at a very high standard of difficulty. The term is used mainly by climbers who do not consistently climb at a very high standard of difficulty.

Tight Rope. A rope held tightly from above to support a climber moving upwards, and to prevent a fall in case the climber slips.

Toe-jam. The wedging of toes in a thin crack to make a foothold. The size of the crack in which toe-jamming is possible depends on the footwear used. With boots, only very wide cracks can be used, but with P.A.'s or rubbers very thin cracks may be used. Toe-jamming can be painful over long stretches.

Toe Traverse. A delicate traverse on small footholds, on which only the toes or the very edge of the feet can be used.

Top Rope. A rope lowered to a leader who is unable to complete a climb without the moral and physical support of a rope from above. On outcrops climbs, it is customary to

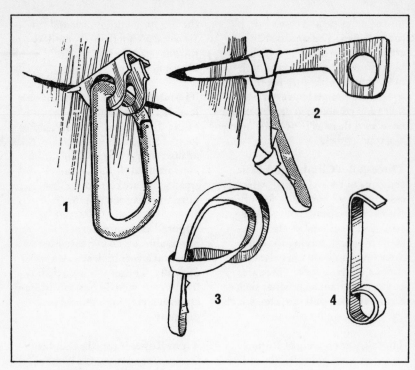

Advanced artificial aids. (1) *Coupled pitons*
(2) *Tied-off piton* (3) *Tie-off knot* (4) *Sky-hook.*

ascend the hardest climbs with the protection of a pre-arranged top rope.

Top-rung Move. Usually a difficult and strenuous manoeuvre in artificial climbing, when the top rung of the étriers has to be used to reach the next crack or piton. On steep walls and overhangs, this throws the climber out of balance, needing considerable arm strength and good technique to sustain the position. (See *Hero Loop.*)

Tor. A hill, often capped with a rocky summit, or a large rounded block of rock on a flat moor, particularly in south-west England and the Pennines.

Tower. A tower of rock often with a flat top; it could be a gendarme or a step on a ridge with a slight gap behind.

Tragsitz. (*German.*) A webbing and canvas seat used to carry an injured climber in mountain rescue operations.

Trail Rope. A spare rope carried by the leader on an artificial climb, which is not clipped into any karabiners. The trail rope can be used for hauling up extra equipment in the middle of a pitch, or for hauling rucksacks with food and bivouac equipment.

Training Climb. A rock climb or a hill-walking excursion in Britain undertaken for practice or to increase ones fitness for more ambitious climbing; a short climb in the Alps undertaken for

acclimatization and to adjust to the larger scale of the mountains.

Traverse. This has several distinct meanings to mountaineers: (1) A horizontal series of movements across a rock face; (2) the crossing of slopes of snow and ice, usually in a diagonal traverse; (3) the ascent and descent of the same mountain by different routes; (4) the crossing of a mountain pass.

When mountains are traversed, as in (3), two ridges are usually followed, but two faces or indeed any two routes count as a traverse so long as they are not too close together.

Traverse In. To gain a route some distance above its start by climbing easier ground on either side and then traversing across to join the route. This is often done on British climbs to avoid dirty or unpleasant pitches near the foot of a cliff.

Traverse Off. To abandon a route by traversing off to either side to join easy ground. This is always possible at some point on artificial climbs. (See *Artificial.*)

Tricouni Nails. Climbing nails made from small steel plates to which one or more serrated edges are fitted by brazing. The serrated edges of the nails afford little friction with the rock, but are very useful for climbing on rough rock with many small holds, as the points can be hooked on to tiny knobs and flakes. Tricouni nails are useful on snow and ice. (See *Nails.*) Diagram p. 85.

Tsampa. Flour of roasted and

*A typical rock climbing pitch. The leader is
belayed to a large flake and is using a waist
belay. The second is on a short traverse above
a roof and is protected by a running belay.*

ground barley or other grain—the staple food of Sherpas.

Tyrolean Traverse. A sensational manoeuvre across a rope fixed between two points and over a considerable drop. This is usually done for a stunt, or for amusement, but the first ascents of some Dolomite pinnacles were made in this way, by lassoing the summit from a nearby rock wall, and swarming across on the rope.

U.I.A.A. *Union Internationale des Associations d' Alpinisme,* founded in 1932 by Egmond d'Arcis, with the object of co-ordinating and fostering mountaineering interests between nations on a world-wide basis. Among the most important works of the organisation, is its aim towards the adoption of international minimum standards for equipment quality and safety and nomenclature and terminology for technical mountaineering publications. The U.I.A.A. has a permanent secretariat and headquarters in Geneva. (See *Dodero Test.*)

Undercut. An undercut handhold, which may be used to assist balance or in opposition to the feet to make an upward movement.

Universal Piton. A piton with an eye twisted to an angle of 45°, so that the piton can be used in the back of vee-grooves. The idea is essentially a compromise in the manufacture of the piton, as the twist is easier to make than a fully forged eye at right angles to the blade, but in practice the pitons work well. Diagram p. 94.

Unzip. A colloquial expression used to describe a fall in artificial climbing, when several pitons are pulled out, one after the other, by the force of the fall.

Vadret. (*German-Italian patois.*) The distinctive name for glaciers in the Bernina Alps, the St. Moritz-Pontresina district of Switzerland. The version used in the Italian half of the Bernina group is *vedretta.*

Vee-chimney. A chimney or deep groove with walls at an acute angle, and which usually meet at the back of the chimney.

Vegetation. Earth, grass, bushes and trees found on a cliff. Many low-lying cliffs in Britain are covered to some extent. (See *Gardening.*)

Ventisquero. (*Spanish.*) The distinctive name for glaciers in the Andes and used for stationary or advancing glaciers, as distinct from *glaciar,* which is used for retreating glaciers.

Verglas. A film of ice on rocks caused by running water freezing and by mist condensing and freezing on the rocks. Verglas is a difficult and sometimes dangerous condition for rock climbing and if the covering is continuous there is little other alternative than to remove it with a piton hammer or ice-axe. Easy rocks covered with verglas may be climbed with crampons. If it is suspected that a route is covered with verglas, the route should be abandoned.

Vertical Piton. A piton which has its eye in the same plane of the blade, so that it can be used in vertical cracks. The concept and the name are out of date, as this type of piton is no longer made. (See *Horizontal Piton*.)

Vibrams. Moulded rubber soles and heels, with an inlaid pattern, which are glued and screwed to the soles of climbing boots. The idea of this type of sole was thought up by Vitale Bramani in 1935. For many years a controversy has raged over the relative merits of Vibrams and nails and it is only recently that Vibrams have been used by mountaineers to the almost total exclusion of nails. The main disadvantages of Vibrams are that they provide little friction on wet rock and slopes of wet grass, but this is far outweighed by the advantages. In fact, even on greasy rocks, Vibrams can be equally effective if the correct techniques are used.

Several weights of Vibram soles are made, for use on lightweight boots and mountain boots. Several types are made with different kinds of rubber, but a softer rubber seems best. Diagram p. 85.

Vire. (*French*.) A ledge of rock or snow of almost any size. A vire can be anything from a normal ledge to a gangway rising steeply across a face.

Volcano. A mountain formed by magma (molten rock) which is forced up through the earth's surface and ejected as lava in cone-shaped deposits. The highest volcanoes in the world are to be found in the Andean chain (Llullaillaco at 22,060 feet is the highest) but there are many notable examples all over the world. Most of the great volcanoes are extinct

and all of them have been climbed.

Waist Belay. Probably the most satisfactory way of taking in and paying out a belayed active rope, by passing the rope around the waist. The hand on the active rope side is the directing hand, the hand on the slack rope side is the controlling hand. The controlling hand usually has a twist of rope around the wrist to increase the friction. The controlling hand is kept securely on the rope all the time and the directing hand is used to feed the rope and control the slack on the ledge. The waist belay is ideal for applying a dynamic belay. Diagram p. 123.

Waistline. A piece of thin rope wound several times around the waist. The ends are knotted with a reef knot and tucked away through the strands. The best type of waistline is made from a 20 foot length of rot-proofed Italian Hemp. The main advantages of a waistline are comfort, greater strength than a single climbing rope and a quicker change-over of positions on the rope, when necessary. A strong screw-gate karabiner is used to attach the climbing rope to the waistline. (See *Harness*.)

Wales. To mountaineers and walkers this means North Wales and especially the Snowdon district (Snowdonia).

Walker. A person who walks up mountains by routes not needing any special techniques or equipment, such as rope. (See *Hill-walking*.)

Wall. A rock face inclined between 75 and 90 degrees to the horizontal,

Belaying. (1) *Waist Belay* (2) *Shoulder Belay.*

though this definition is arbitrary. Wall climbs give strenuous and delicate climbing, usually with a fair amount of exposure.

The name may be used for the entire face of a mountain or the flank of a major ridge on a mountain, e.g. the North Wall of the Eiger.

Water Ice. Ice formed directly by the freezing of water, as opposed to ice formed under pressure. It is brittle and unreliable for cutting steps, and is found mainly in gullies and on rocks.

Wedge. A wedge-shaped piece of wood drilled through one end and a sling attached, and used as a piton for driving into wide cracks. The use of wedges has deteriorated with the recent introduction of the far superior bongs, but they are still useful for extremely wide cracks. (See *Cale* and *Bong-bong*.) Diagram p. 94.

Welsh 3000-footers. The fourteen summits in North Wales which exceed the altitude of 3000 feet. Climbers and cross-country runners frequently make the traverse of all these peaks in a day. The record time for the traverse now stands at about six hours.

White-out. A condition which occurs in bad and misty weather on any snow-covered mountain, when the mist makes it impossible to distinguish features on the ground. This can be very dangerous, as the tops of gullies or the start of steep slopes cannot easily be seen.

Wind-slab. A snow crust, formed by wind-blown snow which settles insecurely on old snow. The crust is usually hard, but is unstable, and tends to break off very easily. Wind-slab can be a very dangerous avalanche condition, particularly in the spring and can be a problem for skiers and climbers alike.

Winter Ascents. Winter climbing in Britain is conditioned by the annual snow-fall and the periods of cold weather. In England and Wales it is largely a matter of luck, whether good snow and ice climbing is possible at all, but in Scotland excellent snow conditions are often found. Winter climbing is especially popular in Glencoe, on Ben Nevis and in the Cairngorms. Winter conditions in Scotland can be extremely bad, and as most of the areas are remote, climbing in winter is a serious undertaking.

Winter climbing in the Alps is regarded by some climbers as being superior to summer climbing. Apart from the fact that the mountains are less crowded, periods of good weather tend to be longer and more settled, snow conditions are much better on average and objective dangers are reduced. Against this must be weighed the very low temperatures, the high winds and the prospect of being caught in intensely bad storms. The winter season in the Alps is clearly defined as far as the 'official' records go, and the ascent of a route outside of this period, even if it be in a hard winter storm, does not count as a winter ascent. The situation has recently been made more ridiculous by the introduction of specific dates of autumn and spring seasons, thus further limiting the 'official' winter season.

Wire Slings. Slings made from high quality wire, joined with a Teleric clip. Wire slings are very useful for sharp flakes which might cut a rope or tape sling, and for using on very small thread belays. Their breaking strain is somewhere in the region of 1000 lbs., depending on the size of wire used.

Wrist Sling. A webbing or leather strap fixed to a sliding metal ring on the shaft of an ice-axe. The sling fits over the wrist to prevent loss of the axe if it is dropped. (See *Ice-axe*.) Diagram p. 70.

Zardsky Sack. One of the original bivouac tents, designed and made in Germany.

Zinne. (*German*). A pointed rock peak, particularly in the Dolomites.

Addenda

Conventional Signs. A system for grading rock climbs and a series of symbols for guide-book diagrams designed by the U.I.A.A. in an attempt to rationalise the technical description of climbs on an international scale. Free rock climbs are graded by Roman numerals (I through VI), with subdivisions of + and − from grade III upwards; artificial climbs are graded A1 through A4, with a suffix of e, when expansion bolts are used. The symbols for diagrams are comprehensive and cover the representation of visible, hidden and variant routes; cracks, chimneys, roofs and other physical features of climbs; ledges, stances and bivouac places, etc. The concept of Conventional Signs is still very much experimental, due to the difficulties of aligning the existing systems in use and the slow production of new guide books, and no doubt the system will be modified in light of future experience.

Dead Man. A snow belay, consisting of a large sheet of aluminium alloy about 9″ square and shaped rather like the blade of a flat shovel. The top edge is reinforced, so that the Dead Man can be hammered into hard snow and the blade has two small holes drilled through it, to which a spliced wire sling is attached. The Dead Man works on the principle that any force on it tends to drive it deeper into the snow. Thus, with correct placement, so that any downward force is greater than the corresponding horizontal force, a satisfactory belay can be arranged even in soft snow and powder snow. The Dead Man is a revolutionary advance in snow belaying techniques, which should have far reaching consequences.

HiTens. A new type of British piton, made from a nickel alloy, with a tensile strength of 125 tons as against the 75 tons of chrome-molybdenum steel. This material gives the pitons a greater holding power and a longer life than any other piton available. Because of the exceptional strength of the alloy, very thin blade pitons can be made, which can be driven into indifferent and blind cracks.

New Zealand snow belay. A modern method of belaying on snow, using only an ice-axe. One hand is used to control and hold the rope, the other hand is used to hold the ice-axe firmly in the snow. Additional friction on the active rope is produced by running the rope around the outside of one boot, firmly planted near the head of the ice-axe. This method of belaying requires practice and a high degree of co-ordination, but it is possible to hold long leader falls by this method.

Appendix 1

*General index of English
and foreign terms*

Items appearing in this index fall into
several categories as follows:
English terms which have the same,
or several, meanings; English
colloquial terms; Welsh and Gaelic
names used for mountain features;
American colloquial expressions;
French, German, Italian and Spanish
terms which might be used
frequently in guide books and other
publications, which have a special
meaning for mountaineers, and
which provide a useful basis for
translation. All the cross-references
are to terms which appear as main
headings in the Dictionary; those in
italics are foreign terms.

Abbreviations:
Fr–French
G–German
It–Italian
Sp–Spanish

*–Colloquial

Acarreo (Sp)	Scree
Adherence (Fr)	Friction
Aguja (Sp)	Pinnacle
Aide Extérieure (Fr)	Top Rope
Anchor	Belay
Anneau de corde (Fr)	Sling
Appiglio (It)	Hold
Appogio (It)	Foothold
Arista (Sp)	Spur
Assurance (Fr)	Belay
Baignoire (Fr)*	Jughandle
Band (G)	*Vire*
Baudrier (Fr)	Harness
Bealach, Beinn (Gaelic)	Mountain
Ben (Scots)	Mountain
Bivacco (It)	Bivouac Hut
Bivak Schachtel (G)	Bivouac Hut
Block coincé (Fr)	Chockstone
Bolt*	Expansion Bolt
Broche (Fr)	Channel Piton
Broche à glace (Fr)	Ice-piton
Broche à vis (Fr)	Ice-screw
Bryn (Welsh)	Hill
Bwlch (Welsh)	High Pass
Cabane (Fr)	Hut
Camino (It)	Chimney
Campanile (It)	*Clocher*
Canale (It)	*Couloir*
Canaletea (Sp)	*Couloir*
Canalone (It)	Large *couloir*
Capanna (It)	Hut
Cengia (It)	*Vire*
Cheminée (Fr)	Chimney
Chimenea (Sp)	Chimney
Chinning (American)	Mantleshelf
Chiodo (It)	Piton
Circo (It)	*Cirque*
Clavo (Sp)	Piton
Clogwyn (Welsh)	Cliff
Coincement (Fr)	Jamming
Coin de bois (Fr)	Wedge

Coire (Gaelic)	*Cirque*
Colatoio (It)	Narrow *couloir*
Colle (It)	Pass
Contrefort (Fr)	Buttress
Corda (It)	Rope
Corda Doppia (It)	*Abseil*
Corde (Fr)	Rope
Cordino (It)	Sling
Corniche (Fr)	Cornice
Cornière (Fr)	Channel Piton
Corrie (Scots)	*Cirque*
Course (Fr)	Route
Courte-échelle (Fr)	Shoulder
Crab*	*Karabiner*
Craig (Celtic)	Crag
Creag (Gaelic)	Crag
Crepaccio (It)	Crevasse
Cresta (It)	*Crête*
Crib (Welsh)	Ridge
Crochet (Fr)	Sky-hook
Cuerda (Sp)	Rope
Cuña (Sp)	Wedge
Cuneo (It)	Wedge
Dalle (Fr)	Slab
Dach (G)	Roof
Dièdre (Fr)	Groove
Dihedral (American)	Groove
Écaille (Fr)	Flake
Éboulis (Fr)	Scree
Eis (G)	Ice
Eisbeil (G)	North-wall hammer
Éperon (Fr)	Spur
Escama (Sp)	Slab
Espolon (Sp)	Spur
Estribo (Sp)	*Étrier*
Extraplomo (Sp)	Overhang
Falaise (Fr)	Cliff
Fessure (Fr)	Crack
Fessura (It)	Crack
Feuillet (Fr)	Flake
Firn (G)	*Névé*

Forcella

Forcella (It)	*Brèche*
Gabel (G)	*Brèche*
Gaiters	*Stoptout*
Geroll (G)	Scree
Ghiaccio (It)	Ice
Ghiacciaio (It)	Glacier
Ghiaioi (It)	Scree
Glace (Fr)	Ice
Gletscher (G)	Glacier
Golo (Fr)*	Expansion Bolt
Grampones (Sp)	*Crampons*
Grat (G)	Ridge
Grattons (Fr)	Small holds
Grava (It)	Scree
Grieta (Sp)	Crevasse
Guglia (It)	Needle
Haken (G)	Pitons
Hanger*	Fish Plate
Hardware*	Ironmongery
Hielo (Sp)	Ice, Ice-field
Hip-Belay	Waist-Belay
Homme de Pierre (Fr)	Cairn
Horquilla (Sp)	*Brèche*
Hutte (G)	Hut
Incastro (It)	Jamming
Intaglia (It)	*Brèche*
Joch (G)	*Col*
Kamin (G)	Chimney
Kamm (G)	Ridge
Kante (G)	Edge, *arête*
Karr (G)	*Cirque*
Klets*	*Kletterschuhe*
Klettergarten (G)	Outcrop
Largo (Sp)	Pitch
Lawine (G)	Avalanche
Lie-back (American)	Layback
Llyn (Welsh)	Lake

Loch

Loch (Gaelic)	Lake
Lochan (Gaelic)	Small lake
Lunghezza (It)	Pitch
Marteau-piolet (Fr)	North-wall hammer
Moat (American)	*Roture*
Morena (It)	Moraine
Moschettone (It)	*Karabiner*
Mousequeton (Fr)	*Karabiner*
Muraglia (It)	Wall
Muraille (Fr)	Wall
Nevaio (It)	*Névé*
Nicchia (It)	Niche
Nieve (Sp)	Snow, *névé*
Opposition (Fr)	Layback, bridging
Palestra di roccia (It)	Outcrop
Pared (Sp)	Wall
Parete (It)	Wall
Paroi (Fr)	Wall
Pentu (Fr)*	Steep
Pfeiler (G)	Pillar
Piaz (G)	Layback
Piccoza (It)	Ice-axe
Pickel (G)	Ice-axe
Pierrier (Fr)	Scree
Pilastro (It)	Pillar
Pilier (Fr)	Pillar
Pin*	Piton
Piolet (Fr)	Ice-axe
Pit*	Sleeping Bag
Piton-en-U (Fr)	Channel Piton
Piqueta (Sp)	Ice-axe
Placce (It)	Slab
Plaque (Fr)	Smooth wall or slab
Platte (G)	Slab
Ponte Naturale (It)	Natural Thread
Prise (Fr)	Hold
Punto di Sosta (It)	Stance
Quergang (G)	Traverse

Ramasse

Ramasse (Fr)	Glissade
Ramonage (Fr)	Bridging (in chimneys)
Ramponi (It)	*Crampons*
Rappel (Fr)	*Abseil*
Refuge (Fr)	Hut
Refuge-bivouac (Fr)	Bivouac Hut
Relais (Fr)	Stance
Relais (Fr)*	Pitch
Relevo (Sp)	Belay
Retablissement (Fr)	Mantleshelf
Rib-riding (American)	À cheval
Rifugio (It)	Hut
Rimaye (Fr)	*Bergschrund*
Sanduhr (G)	Natural Thread
Sangle (Fr)	Tape
Sattel (G)	Saddle
Scanalature (It)	*Cannelures*
Scharte (G)	*Col*
Schrund (G)	Crevasse
Seil (G)	Rope
Sella (It)	Large *col*
Sicurezza (It)	Belay
Slievh (Irish)	Mountain
Sgurr (Gaelic)	Rock peak
Snap-link	*Karabiner*
Sperone (It)	Spur
Spigolo (It)	Edge, *arête*
Spitze (G)	Peak
Square knot (American)	Reef knot
Staffa (It)	*Étrier*
Standplatz (G)	Stance
Steigeisen (G)	*Crampons*
Steigleiter (G)	*Étrier*
Stirrup (American)	*Étrier*
Strapiombo (It)	Overhang
Surplomb (Fr)	Overhang
Tal (G)	Valley
Talus (American)	Scree
Tapes (American)	*Étriers*
Techo (Sp)	Roof
Terrazza (It)	Platform

Tetto

Tetto (It)	Roof
Thorl (G)	Narrow pass
Tiro di corda (It)	*Longeur*
Toit (Fr)	Roof
Tomas (Sp)	Holds
Valanga (It)	Avalanche
Varappe (Fr)	Scramble
Verrou (Fr)	Wedge (jam)
Verschneidung (G)	Groove
Vetrato (It)	Verglas
Via (It)	Route
Voie (Fr)	Route
Wand (G)	Wall
Webbing	Tape
Weg (G)	Route
Zoccollo (It)	*Socle*

Appendix 2

*A survey of climbing guide books
in English (1968)*

These guide books are single
volumes, except where stated, whose
pages cover not only the area
suggested in each title, but also the
surrounding and outlying ground to
each area. All of them have been
published or re-edited recently,
except where indicated.

Lake District
Published by the *Fell and Rock
Climbing Club*
Great Langdale
Eastern Crags
Scafell
Published privately
Borrowdale
in preparation
Great Gable
Pillar Rock
Buttermere
Dow Crag

North Wales
Published by the *Climber's Club*
Carneddau
Cwm Idwal
Tryfan and Glyder Fach
Llanberis North
Llanberis South
Clogwyn du'r Arddu
Lliwedd (1946)
Snowdon South
in preparation
Snowdon West
Snowdon East
Published privately
Craig Gogarth

Scotland
Published by the *Scottish
Mountaineering Club*
The Cullin of Skye
Glencoe (2 vols)

Cairngorms (2 vols)
Arran
in preparation
Arrochar
Ben Nevis
Northern Highlands (3 vols.)
Isle of Skye (2 vols.)
Published privately
Easter Ross
Foinavon
Creag Meaghaidh
Carnmore

Peak District and Yorkshire
Published by Cade & Co. for the
British Mountaineering Council
Sheffield-Stanage Area
Chew Valley and Laddow Area
Sheffield-Froggatt Area
in preparation
Chatsworth and Matlock Areas
Bleaklow and Kinder Scout
Roches and Churnet Areas
Published privately
The Mountain Limestone of
Derbyshire
Derwent Valley Limestone
Stoney Middleton Dale
North Yorkshire Moors
Yorkshire Limestone
Roches and Hen Cloud

Northern England and Midlands
Published privately
Northumberland
Helsby Rocks
Pontesford Rocks
Leicestershire Area

Southern England
Published by the *Climber's Club*
South East England
Cornwall (2 vols)
Published privately
Limestone climbs on the Dorset
Coast
Wye Valley and the Cotswolds

South West England
Devonshire

Isle of Man
Fell Walking and Climbing guide to
the Isle of Man

Ireland
Published by the *Irish Mountaineering
Club*
Mourne Rock Climbs (1958)
Dalkey Quarry
Donegal
Glendalough (1957)
Glen Inagh

The Alps
Published by the *Alpine Club*
Mont Blanc Range (2 vols.)
Pennine Alps (2 vols.)
Dolomites
Dauphiné Alps and Vercours
Bernese Alps
Published by *West Col Productions*
Bregaglia West
Dents du Midi
Graians West
Engelhorner and Salbitschijen
Maritime Alps
Bernina Alps
Many other guide books in English
are published, notably those to
Mt. Kenya and Kilimanjaro, Table
Mountain, Gibraltar, Norway,
Yosemite and other areas in North
America. A further title of
particular interest to British
climbers is *Where to Climb in the
British Isles,* by E. C. Pyatt (Faber,
1960), which gives details of all
outcrops and mountain crags in the
country.

Appendix 3

Technical books on climbing

A list of books and booklets, published in the English language, which describe in varying degrees of detail the technique of climbing mountains. Many of the earlier editions are unavailable, except through private collections and club libraries, but are included from historical interest and completeness.

Mountaineering (Badminton Library)
C. T. Dent, Ed. 1892

Mountaineering (Methuen)
C. Wilson 1893

The Complete Mountaineer
G. D. Abraham 1907

British Mountaineering
C. E. Benson 1909

Mountain Craft
G. W. Young 1920

Mountaineering Art
H. Raeburn 1920

First Steps to Climbing
G. D. Abraham 1924

The Art of Mountain Tramping
R. W. Hall 1932

The Complete Hill Walker, Rock Climber and Cave Explorer
W. T. Palmer 1934

Mountaineering (Lonsdale Library)
S. Spencer, Ed. 1934

The Technique of Alpine Mountaineering
E. A. M. Wedderburn, Ed. 1935

Appendix 3

Alpine Climbing on Foot and with Ski
E. A. M. Wedderburn 1936

Mountaineering (A. & C. Black)
T. A. H. Peacocke 1941

Let's Go Climbing
C. F. Kirkus 1941

Handbook of American Mountaineering
K. A. Henderson, Ed. 1942

Rock Climbing and Mountaineering
C. Brunning 2nd ed. 1946

Climbing in Britain
J. E. Q. Barford, Ed. 1946

A Short Manual of Mountaineering Training
W. C. Burns, F. Shuttleworth, J. E. B. Wright 1948

Progress in Mountaineering
J. H. B. Bell 1950

The Mountaineering Handbook
A.B.M.S.A.C. 1950

Elementary Mountaineering
Mountaineering Association 1951

The Technique of Mountaineering
J. E. B. Wright 1955

An Introduction to Mountaineering
Showell Styles 1955

Nylon Rope and Climbing Safety
K. Tarbuk 1955

Come Climbing With Me
R. W. Clark 1955

On Climbing
R. C. Evans 1956

Getting to Know Mountains
Showell Styles 1958

Tackle Climbing This Way
J. Disley 1959

Safety on Mountains
C.C.P.R. 1961

Artificial Aids in Mountaineering
G. J. Sutton 1962

Instructions in Rock Climbing
A. Greenbank 1963

Rock Climbing
P. Nock 1963

On Snow and Rock
G. Rébuffat 1963

Rock Climbing (Know the Game Series)
C. M. Dixon 1964

Mountain Climbing
G. H. Francis 2nd ed. 1964

Mountaineering (Penguin Handbook)
A. Blackshaw 1965

If any of the above titles should be singled out for particular mention, then one could recommend *Mountain Craft* (G. W. Young, 1920—revised 1949) and the 1965 Penguin Handbook *Mountaineering*, by A. Blackshaw, both of which are classics.

Appendix 4

Magazines and Journals

The following publications are all recommended to British climbers. The magazines are obtainable from climbing equipment shops, as are some of the club journals. The continental club journals are usually only available to members, or by direct application. There are many more journals and newsletters produced by British mountaineering clubs, some of which are high quality publications, but these are usually only available to club members and tend to be of a limited interest.

General Magazines

Mountaineering, British Mountaineering Council, bi-annual.
Mountain Craft, Mountaineering Association, quarterly.
The Climber, George Outram Ltd., monthly.
Rocksport, Ainsworth and Watkin, two monthly
Alpinismus, Heering-Verlag GmbH, Munich, monthly.
Summit, J. M. Crenshaw, California, monthly.
Ascent, Sierra Mountaineering Club, annual.

Club Magazines

Alpine Climbing, Alpine Climbing Group, annual.
Les Alpes (Die Alpen), Swiss Alpine Club, monthly and quarterly.
La Montagne, French Alpine Club and Groupe de Haute Montagne, quarterly.
Les Annales du G.H.M., Groupe de Haute Montagne, annual.
Revista Mensile, Italian Alpine Club, monthly.

New Climbs, Climber's Club,
annual.

Club Journals
Alpine Journal, The Alpine Club,
bi-annual.
Climber's Club Journal, The
Climber's Club, annual.
Fell and Rock Journal, Fell and Rock
Climbing Club, annual.
Irish Mountaineering Club Journal,
Irish Mountaineering Club, annual.
Rucksack Club Journal, Rucksack
Club, annual.
Scottish Mountaineering Club Journal,
Scottish Mountaineering Club,
annual.
American Alpine Club Journal,
American Alpine Club, annual.
Himalayan Club Journal, Himalayan
Club, annual.
also:
Mountain World, Allen and Unwin,
on behalf of the Swiss Foundation
for Alpine Research, annual.

Notes

Notes